Clas

Fiction and Poetry Texts

Eileen Jones

Text © Eileen Jones 2004
Original illustrations © Nelson Thornes Ltd 2004

The right of Eileen Jones to be identified as author of this work has been asserted by her in accordance with the Copyright, Designs and Patents Act 1988.

All rights reserved. The copyright holders authorise ONLY users of *Classworks Fiction and Poetry Texts Year 6* to make photocopies of *pages 5–54* for their own or their students' immediate use within the teaching context. No other rights are granted without permission in writing from the publishers or under licence from the Copyright Licensing Agency Limited. Further details of such licences (for reprographic reproduction) may be obtained from the Copyright Licensing Agency Limited, of 90 Tottenham Court Road, London W1T 4LP.

Copy by any other means or for any other purpose is strictly prohibited without prior written consent from the copyright holders. Application for such permission should be addressed to the publishers.

Any person who commits any unauthorised act in relation to this publication may be liable to criminal prosecution and civil claims for damages.

Published in 2004 by:
Nelson Thornes Ltd
Delta Place
27 Bath Road
CHELTENHAM
GL53 7TH
United Kingdom

04 05 06 07 08 / 10 9 8 7 6 5 4 3 2 1

A catalogue record for this book is available from the British Library

ISBN 0-7487-8651-1

Illustrations by Martha Hardy and Lisa Williams
Page make-up by GreenGate Publishing Services

Printed in Great Britain by Ashford Colour Press

Acknowledgements
All texts written by Eileen Jones except:

'Who Knows' from *Please Mrs Butler* by Allan Ahlberg (Kestral, 1983) copyright © Allan Ahlberg, 1983; 'It is a Puzzle' from *Please Mrs Butler* by Allan Ahlberg (Kestral, 1983) copyright © Allan Ahlberg, 1983; 'For Word' from *Funky Chickens* by Benjamin Zephaniah (Viking, 1996) copyright © Benjamin Zephaniah 1996; 'Pencil Me In' from *Funky Chickens* by Benjamin Zephaniah (Viking, 1996) copyright © Benjamin Zephaniah 1996; *Why the Whales Came* text copyright © Michael Morpurgo 1995. Published by Egmont Books Ltd, London and used with permission. *The Sheep-Pig* by Dick King-Smith (Victor Gollancz/Hamish Hamilton, 1983) copyright © Dick King-Smith, 1983; *The Hundred and One Dalmations* used by kind permission of Julian Barnes, executor of the estate of the late Dodie Smith and Brendan Davis, Agent of Laurence Fitch Ltd for the estate of the late Dodie Smith; Extract from *Peter Pan* copyright © 1937 Great Ormond Street Hospital for Children, London; *Peter Pan (the motion picture event)* copyright © Simon and Schuster; *The Witches* by Roald Dahl reproduced by permission of David Higham Associates copyright © Roald Dahl 1983; *The Witches* taken from *The Witches: Plays for Children* by Roald Dahl and David Wood reproduced by permission of David Higham Associates Copyright © Roald Dahl and David Wood 2001; Extract from *The Story of Tracy Beaker* by Jacqueline Wilson published by Corgi Yearling. Used by permission of Random House Group Limited; Extract from *My Friend Walter* text copyright © Michael Morpurgo 1988. Published by Egmont Books Limited, London and used with permission; *Mrs Frisby and the Rats of Nimh* by Robert O'Brien copyright © Robert O'Brien; *When Hitler Stole Pink Rabbit* reprinted by permission of HarperCollins Ltd Copyright © Judith Kerr 1971; Extract from *Charlotte Sometimes* by Penelope Farmer published by Bodley Head. Used by permission of Random House Group Ltd; *The Borrowers* by Mary Norton reproduced by permission of Orion Publishing Group Ltd copyright © Mary Norton 1952; Extracts from *Shadow of the Minotaur* by Alan Gibbons. Reproduced by permission of Orion Children's Books. Copyright © Alan Gibbons 2000; Extract from *Moon Cake* taken from *Moon Cake and Other Stories* by Joan Aiken. Reproduced by permission of Hodder and Stoughton Limited. Copyright © Joan Aiken 1998; 'Dawlish Dobson' taken from *I want to be an Angel* by Jamila Gavin reproduced by permission of David Higham Associates. Copyright © Jamila Gavin 1998; 'The Road Not Taken' by Robert Frost from *The Poetry of Robert Frost*, edited by Edward Connery Lathem and published by Jonathan Cape. Used by permission of the Estate of Robert Frost and The Random House Group Limited; 'The Donkey' by G K Chesterton; *The Mouse and his Child* copyright © Russell Hoban; Extract from *Magnus Powermouse* by Dick King-Smith. Reproduced by permission of A P Watt Literary Agents, 20 John Street, London, WC1N 2DR. Copyright © Dick King-Smith 1982; Extract from *The Amazing Maurice and his Educated Rodents* by Terry and Lyn Pratchett published by Doubleday. Used by permission of Transworld Publishers, a division of The Random House Group Limited; *The War of Jenkins Ear* text copyright © Michael Morpurgo 1993. Published by Egmont Books Ltd, London and used with permission; *Harry Potter and the Order of the Phoenix* copyright © J K Rowling 2003; *Goodnight Mr Tom* by Michelle Magorian (Kestral, 1981) copyright © Michelle Magorian, 1981.

Cover image: AA025496 © Getty/Photodisc Green/Mel Curtis (royalty free) Close-up of Angel, Hanno

Every effort has been made to trace the copyright holders but if any have been inadvertently overlooked, the publishers will be pleased to make the necessary arrangement at the first opportunity.

Contents

How to use this book 4

Texts 5–54

TERM 1

Poetry
1. Who Knows? *Allan Ahlberg*
2. It is a Puzzle *Allan Ahlberg*
3. For Word *Benjamin Zephaniah*
4. Pencil Me In *Benjamin Zephaniah*

Narrative writing 1
5. Why the Whales Came (1) *Michael Morpurgo*
6. The Sheep-Pig (1) *Dick King-Smith*
7. The Hundred and One Dalmatians *Dodie Smith*

Media and plays
8. Peter Pan and Wendy *J M Barrie*
9. Peter Pan (the motion picture event) *J M Barrie*
10. The Witches *Roald Dahl*
11. The Witches: Plays for Children *Roald Dahl and David Wood*

Narrative writing 2
12. The Story of Tracy Beaker *Jacqueline Wilson*
13. My Friend Walter *Michael Morpurgo*
14. Mrs Frisby and the Rats of Nimh *Robert O'Brien*
15. When Hitler Stole Pink Rabbit *Judith Kerr*
16. The Sheep-Pig (2) *Dick King-Smith*

TERM 2

Poetry
17. Jabberwocky *Lewis Carroll*
18. The Witches' Chant *Roald Dahl*
19. Fire, Burn; and Cauldron, Bubble *William Shakespeare*

Narrative 1
20. Charlotte Sometimes (1) *Penelope Farmer*
21. Charlotte Sometimes (2) *Penelope Farmer*
22. The Borrowers *Mary Norton*
23. Alice Through the Looking Glass *Lewis Carroll*
24. The Story of Zoe *Eileen Jones*

Narrative 2
25. What Katy Did (1) *Susan Coolidge*
26. Five Children and It (1) *E Nesbit*
27. Shadow of the Minotaur (1) *Alan Gibbons*
28. What Katy Did (2) *Susan Coolidge*
29. Five Children and It (2) *E Nesbit*
30. Shadow of the Minotaur (2) *Alan Gibbons*

TERM 3

Reading and writing narrative
31. Moon Cake *Joan Aiken*
32. Dawlish Dobson *Jamila Gavin*
33. The Journey *Eileen Jones*

Poetry
34. Annus Mirabilis *John Dryden*
35. Again *Eileen Jones*
36. The Road Not Taken *Robert Frost*
37. The Donkey *G K Chesterton*
38. Escape at Bedtime *Robert Louis Stevenson*
39. The Moon *Robert Louis Stevenson*
40. The Moon *Emily Dickinson*
41. Evening *Emily Dickinson*

Authors and texts
42. Black Beauty *Anna Sewell*
43. Why the Whales Came (2) *Michael Morpurgo*
44. The Mouse and his Child *Russell Hoban*
45. Magnus Powermouse *Dick King-Smith*
46. The Amazing Maurice and His Educated Rodents *Terry and Lyn Pratchett*

Extended narrative
47. The War of Jenkins' Ear *Michael Morpurgo*
48. Harry Potter and the Order of the Phoenix *J K Rowling*
49. Changing Places *Eileen Jones*
50. Goodnight Mr Tom *Michelle Magorian*

Teaching notes and ideas 55–64

How to use this book

What this book contains

- Extracts from published works, plus tailor-made extracts, all arranged and chosen specifically to match the examples of medium-term planning provided by the National Literacy Strategy
- Teaching ideas for each extract to get you started, covering some of the relevant text, sentence or word level objectives from the relevant unit

How you can use *Classworks Literacy Texts* with other resources

- The blocked unit structure means you can dip into the book to find resources perfect for what you're teaching this week – it doesn't matter what plan, scheme or other resource you're using
- There are two *Classworks Literacy Texts* books for every year from Reception (or Primary 1) to Year 6 (or Primary 7): one contains Fiction and Poetry, the other contains Non-fiction. Both books together contain texts for every unit of the medium-term plans

What each page does

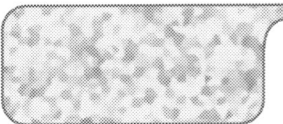

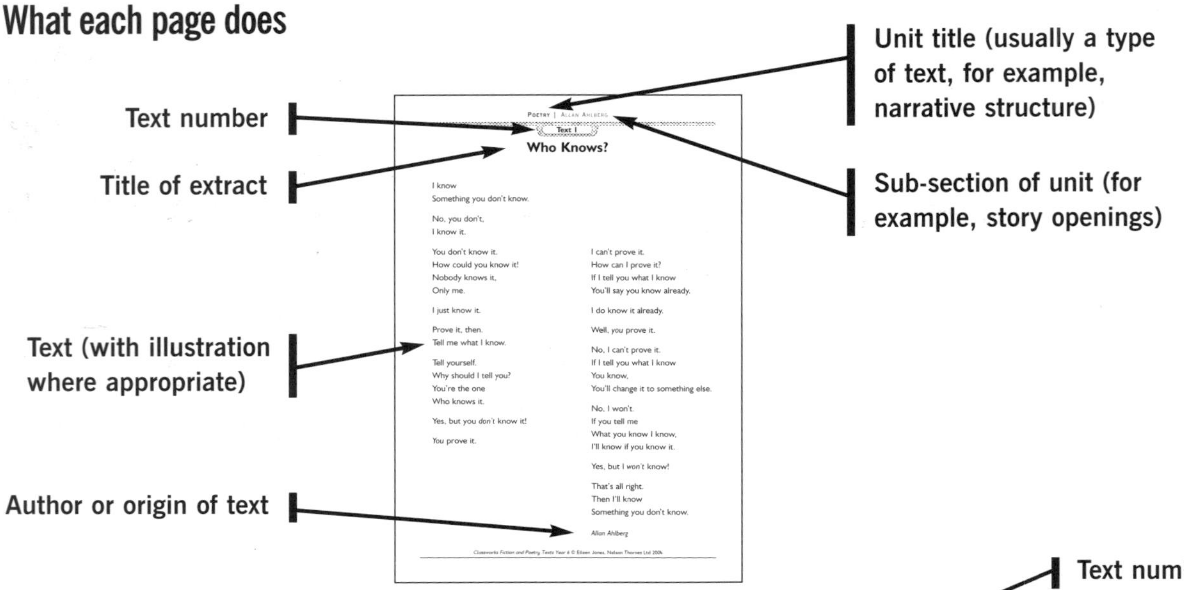
Text number
Title of extract
Text (with illustration where appropriate)
Author or origin of text
Unit title (usually a type of text, for example, narrative structure)
Sub-section of unit (for example, story openings)
Text 1
Who Knows?

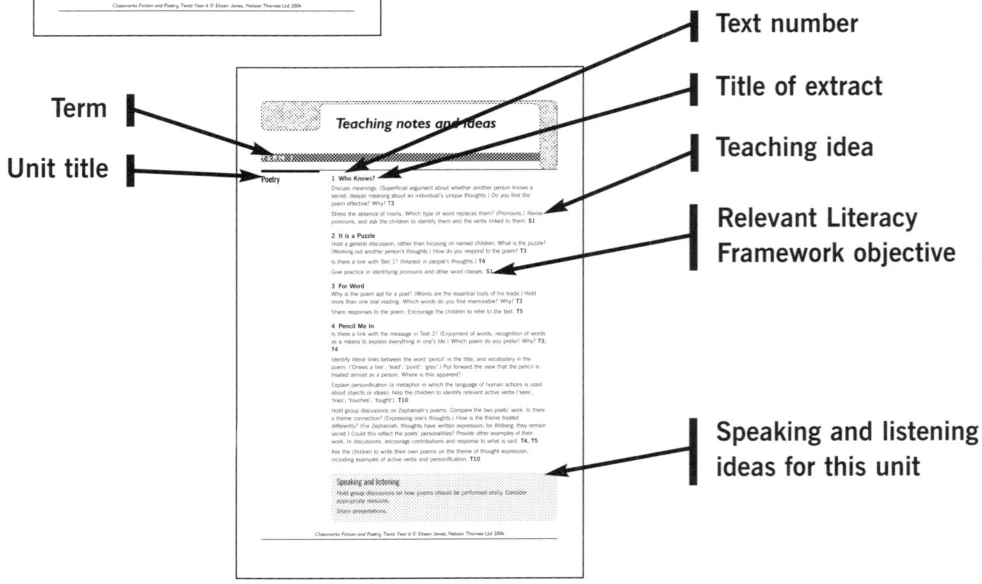
Term
Unit title
Teaching notes and ideas
Text number
Title of extract
Teaching idea
Relevant Literacy Framework objective
Speaking and listening ideas for this unit

Who Knows?

I know
Something you don't know.

No, you don't,
I know it.

You don't know it.
How could you know it!
Nobody knows it,
Only me.

I just know it.

Prove it, then.
Tell me what I know.

Tell yourself.
Why should I tell you?
You're the one
Who knows it.

Yes, but you *don't* know it!

You prove it.

I can't prove it.
How can I prove it?
If I tell you what I know
You'll say you know already.

I do know it already.

Well, *you* prove it.

No, I can't prove it.
If I tell you what I know
You know,
You'll change it to something else.

No, I won't.
If you tell me
What you know I know,
I'll know if you know it.

Yes, but I *won't* know!

That's all right.
Then I'll know
Something you don't know.

Allan Ahlberg

It is a Puzzle

My friend
Is not my friend anymore.
She has secrets from me
And goes about with Tracy Hackett.

I would
Like to get her back,
Only do not want to say so.
So I pretend
To have secrets from her
And go about with Alice Banks.

But what bothers me is,
Maybe *she* is pretending
And would like *me* back,
Only does not want to say so.

In which case
Maybe it bothers her
That *I* am pretending.

But if we are both pretending,
Then really we are friends
And do not know it.

On the other hand,
How can we be friends
And have secrets from each other
And go about with other people?

My friend
Is not my friend anymore,
Unless she is pretending.
I cannot think what to do.
It is a puzzle.

Allan Ahlberg

For Word

Thank you

Thank you for the *words* I read
Thank you for the **words** I need
Thank you for the **WORDS** so great
Thanks for **words** that raise debate,
Thanks for the *words* on my bookshelf
Thanx for the **words** I make myself
Thank you for *words* that make me cry
And *words* that leave me feeling dry.

Thanks for **WORDS** that do inspire
And those words that burn like fire
Thanks for all the *words* I note
Thank you for all the **words** I quote,
I thank you for the *words* like me
Thanks for **WORDS** that set me free
And I thank you for *words* like you
I always need a *word* or two.

Thanks for **words** that make things plain
And words that help me to explain
Thanks for **words** that make life fun
And *words* that help me overcome,
Thanks for **words** that make me rap
Thanks for **words** that make me clap
Thanks for *words* that make me smile
Thanks for **WORDS** with grace and style.

Thanks for all those **words** that sing
Thanks for *words* are everything
Thanks for all the **WORDS** like this
And little sloppy *words* like kiss,
Thanks for **words** like hip-hooray
And those cool *words* I like to say
Thanks for **words** that reach and touch
Thank you very, very much.

Benjamin Zephaniah

Pencil Me In

I know a pencil
Full of lead,
It knows the thoughts
Within my head,
It knows my secrets
And my fears,
It draws a line
Right through my tears.
I know a pencil
Old and grey,
Willing to work
Both night and day,
Fat and lovely
Light and fine,
It moves with me
Through space and time.

Be they good
Or be they bad,
It tells of all
The dreams I have,
And when I have
No oar to row,
It writes a way
And lets me go.
When baby words
Are crying loud,
It touches words
And makes me proud,
A work of art
It is no fake,
It really has
A point to make.

This pencil sees
The best of me,
The worst
And all the rest
Of me,
And as I go
Through puberty,
It changes all my
Poetry.
It goes with me
On all my tours,
It fought with me
In all word wars,
And peacefully
This pencil tries
To help me learn
And make me wise.

Every pencil needs a hand
And every mind needs to expand,
I know a pencil,
What you see
Is me and it
In harmony.

Benjamin Zephaniah

Why the Whales Came (1)

"YOU KEEP AWAY FROM THE BIRDMAN, GRACIE," my father had warned me often enough. "Keep well clear of him, you hear me now?" And we never would have gone anywhere near him, Daniel and I, had the swans not driven us away from the pool under Gweal Hill where we always went to sail our boats.

Daniel and I had built between us an entire fleet of little boats. Fourteen of them there were, each one light blue with a smart white stripe along the bulwarks. I remember well the warm spring day when we took them down to the pool in father's wheelbarrow. We had just the gentle, constant breeze we needed for a perfect day's sailing. We launched them one by one and then ran round to the far side of the pool to wait for them to come in. It was while we were waiting that a pair of swans came flying over, circled once and then landed in the middle of the pool, sending out great waves in their wake. Two of our boats keeled over and some were eventually washed back to the shore; but we had to wade in after the others to retrieve them. We tried shouting at the swans, we even threw sticks at them; but nothing we did would frighten them away. They simply ignored us, and cruised serenely around the pool, preening themselves. In the end it was we who had to leave, piling our boats into the wheelbarrow and trudging defeated and dejected home to tea.

For some days after that we tried to occupy our pool again, but the swans always seemed to be on the look-out for us and would come gliding towards us in a meaningful, menacing kind of way. They left us in no doubt that they did not want us there, and that they would not be prepared to share the pool with anyone.

So reluctantly we gave up and took our boats to nearby Popplestone Bay, but we found it was so windy there that even on the calmest of days our boats would be capsized or beached almost as soon as we pushed them out. And then one day the fastest boat in the fleet, *Cormorant* it was, was carried out to sea before we could do anything about it. The last we saw of her was the top of her yellow sail as she vanished in the trough of a wave. That was the last straw. After that we never sailed our boats from Popplestone Bay again. We were forced to look for somewhere else.

The beach on the sheltered coast of the island opposite Tresco would have been perfect, for the water was calmer here than anywhere else around the island, but there was always too much happening there. It was the hub of the island. Fishing boats were for ever coming in and going out, leaving great tidal waves behind them big enough to swamp our boats; and the children were often fishing off the quay or splashing through the shallows. Then there were Daniel's brothers and sisters, most of whom always seemed to be on that beach mending nets and lobster pots or painting boats. Of all of them, the one we most wanted to avoid was Big Tim, Daniel's eldest brother, and our chief tormentor; and he was always there.

Michael Morpurgo

The Sheep-Pig (1)

Despite himself, Babe was caught up in the press of jostling bleating animals and carried along with them. Around him rose a chorus of panting protesting voices, some shrill, some hoarse, some deep and guttural, but all saying the same thing.

"Wolf! Wolf!" cried the flock in dazed confusion.

Small by comparison and short in the leg, Babe soon fell behind the main body, and as they reached the top of the hill he found himself right at the back in company with an old sheep who cried "Wolf!" more loudly than any.

"Ma!" he cried breathlessly. "It's you!"

Behind them one dog lay down at a whistle, and in front the flock checked as the other dog steadied them. In the corner of the field the tailboard and wings of the cattle-lorry filled the gateway, and the two men waited, sticks and arms outspread.

"Oh hullo, young un," puffed the old sheep.

"Fine day you chose to come, I'll say."

"What is it? What's happening? Who are these men?" asked Babe.

"Rustlers," said Ma. "They'm sheep-rustlers."

"What d'you mean?"

"Thieves, young un, that's what I do mean. Sheep-stealers. We'll all be in thik lorry afore you can blink your eye."

"What can we do?"

"Do? Ain't nothing we can do, unless we can slip past theseyer wolf."

She made as if to escape, but the dog behind darted in, and she turned back.

Again, one of the men whistled, and the dog pressed. Gradually, held against the headland of the field by the second dog and the men, the flock began to move forward. Already the leaders were nearing the tailboard of the lorry.

"We'm beat," said Ma mournfully. "You run for it, young un." I will, thought Babe, but not the way you mean. Little as he was, he felt suddenly not fear but anger, furious anger that the boss's sheep were being stolen. My mum's not here to protect them so I must, he said to himself bravely, and he ran quickly round the hedge side of the flock, and jumping on to the bottom of the tailboard, turned to face them.

"Please!" he cried. "I beg you! Please don't come any further. If you would be so kind, dear sensible sheep!" His unexpected appearance had a number of immediate effects. The shock of being so politely addressed stopped the flock in its tracks, and the cries of "Wolf!" changed to murmurs of "In't he lovely!" and "Proper little gennulman!" Ma had told them something of her new friend, and now to see him in the flesh and to hear his well-chosen words released them from the dominance of the dogs. They began to fidget and look about for an escape route. This was opened for them when the men (cursing quietly, for above all things they were anxious to avoid too much noise) sent the flanking dog to drive the pig away, and some of the sheep began to slip past them.

Next moment all was chaos. Angrily the dog ran at Babe, who scuttled away squealing at the top of his voice in a mixture of fright and fury. The men closed on him, sticks raised. Desperately he shot between the legs of one, who fell with a crash, while the other, striking out madly, hit the rearguard dog as it came to help, and sent it yowling. In half a minute the carefully planned raid was ruined, as the sheep scattered everywhere.

"Keep yelling, young un!" bawled Ma, as she ran beside Babe. "They won't never stop here with that row going on!"

Dick King-Smith

The Hundred and One Dalmations

Pongo could fight on no longer. Sleep came to him while he thought he was still arguing. Missis waited a few minutes, then crept out and pulled hay round Pongo to hide him. She no longer felt sleepy; she was far too anxious. Even her appetite had gone for the moment. Still, she knew she must find food for them both – and she had no idea how to, for she was almost sure there was no dog anywhere near to help her. But pretending to Pongo that she felt brave had made her really feel a little braver and her tail was no longer down.

She could still see the thatched cottages and she noticed some hens at the back of them. Perhaps the hens would have some stale crusts that she could – well, borrow. She went back.

The first cottage she reached was the one where the little boy lived. And now he was at the back, staring at her! This time, he had an even larger slab of bread and butter, with some jam on it. He ran towards her, holding it out.

"Perhaps he really means it now," thought Missis. "Perhaps he's sorry he hurt Pongo." And she went forward hopefully – though well prepared to dodge stones.

The child waited until she was quite close. Then again he stooped for a stone. But he was on a patch of grass, with no stones handy. So, instead, he threw the slab of bread and butter. He threw it with rage, not love, but that made it no less valuable. Missis caught it neatly and bolted.

"Bless me," she thought, "he's just a small human who likes throwing things. His parents should buy him a ball."

She took the bread and butter back to the haystack and laid it down by her sleeping husband's nose. So far, she had not even licked it, but now she let herself nibble off one very small corner. It tasted so glorious that her appetite came back with a rush, but she left all the rest for Pongo to find when he woke. Again she pulled the hay round him, and then ran to the road. But she saw a man outside the cottage where the little boy lived so she did not dare to go back to visit the hens. She ran in the opposite direction.

It was now a very beautiful winter morning. Every blade of grass was silvered with hoar frost and glittering in the newly-risen sun. But Missis was far too worried to enjoy the beauty. The triumph of getting the bread was wearing off and all sorts of fears were rushing at her.

Suppose Pongo was seriously injured? Suppose he was too lame to go on? Suppose she could find no food close at hand? If she had to go far, she knew she would get lost. She even got lost in Regent's Park, almost every time the Dearlys were off the leash. They often laughed at the way she would stand still, wildly staring round for them. Suppose she never found her way back to Pongo and he searched and searched and never found her? Lost dog! The very words were terrible!

And was she, even now, quite sure of her way back to the haystack?

"It isn't fair," thought Missis. "No one as worried as I am ought to feel hungry, too." For she was ravenous – *and* thirsty. She tried licking the ice in a ditch but it hurt her tongue without quenching her thirst.

She was beginning to think she must go back and make sure where the haystack was, when she came to an old red-brick archway leading to a long gravel drive.

Dodie Smith

Peter Pan and Wendy

Peter gave the signal, and the carrion was cast overboard. There was a splash, and then silence. How long has it taken? "One!" (Slightly had begun to count.)

None too soon, Peter, every inch of him on tip-toe, vanished into the cabin; for more than one pirate was screwing up his courage to look round. They could hear each other's distressed breathing now, which showed them that the more terrible sound had passed.

"It's gone, captain," Smee said, wiping his spectacles. "All's still again."

Slowly Hook let his head emerge from his ruff, and listened so intently that he could have caught the echo of the tick. There was not a sound, and he drew himself up firmly to his full height.

"Then here's to Johnny Plank!" he cried brazenly, hating the boys more than ever because they had seen him unbend. He broke into the villainous ditty:

> "Yo ho, yo ho, the frisky plank,
> You walks along it so,
> Till it goes down and you goes down
> To Davy Jones below!"

To terrorise the prisoners the more, though with a certain loss of dignity, he danced along an imaginary plank, grimacing at them as he sang; and when he finished he cried, "Do you want a touch of the cat before you walk the plank?"

At that they fell on their knees. "No, no!" they cried so piteously that every pirate smiled.

"Fetch the cat, Jukes," said Hook, "it's in the cabin."

The cabin! Peter was in the cabin!

The children gazed at each other.

"Ay, ay," said Jukes blithely, and he strode into the cabin. They followed him with their eyes; they scarce knew that Hook had resumed his song, his dogs joining in with him:

> "Yo ho, yo ho, the scratching cat,
> Its tails are nine, you know,
> And when they're writ upon your back – "

What was the last line will never be known, for of a sudden the song was stayed by a dreadful screech from the cabin. It wailed through the ship, and died away. Then was heard a crowing sound which was well understood by the boys, but to the pirates was almost more eerie than the screech.

"What was that?" cried Hook.

"Two," said Slightly solemnly.

The Italian Cecco hesitated for a moment and then swung into the cabin. He tottered out, haggard.

"What's the matter with Bill Jukes, you dog?" hissed Hook, towering over him.

"The matter wi' him is he's dead, stabbed," replied Cecco in a hollow voice.

"Bill Jukes dead!" cried the startled pirates.

"The cabin's as black as a pit," Cecco said, almost gibbering, "but there is something terrible in there: the thing you heard crowing."

The exultation of the boys, the lowering looks of the pirates, both were seen by Hook.

"Cecco," he said in his most steely voice, "go back and fetch me out that doodle-doo"

Cecco, bravest of the brave, cowered before his captain, crying, "No, no"; but Hook was purring to his claw.

"Did you say you would go, Cecco?" he said musingly.

Cecco went, first flinging up his arms despairingly. There was no more singing, all listened now; and again came a death-screech and again a crow.

No one spoke except Slightly. "Three," he said.

Hook rallied his dogs with a gesture.

"'Sdeath and odds fish," he thundered, "who is to bring me that doodle-doo?"

"Wait till Cecco comes out," growled Starkey, and the others took up the cry.

"I think I heard you volunteer, Starkey," said Hook, purring again.

"No, by thunder!" Starkey cried.

"My hook thinks you did," said Hook, crossing to him. "I wonder if it would be advisable, Starkey, to humour the hook?"

"I'll swing before I go in there," replied Starkey doggedly, and again he had the support of the crew.

"Is it mutiny?" asked Hook more pleasantly than ever. "Starkey's ring-leader!"

"Captain, mercy!" Starkey whimpered, all of a tremble now.

"Shake hands, Starkey," said Hook, proffering his claw.

Starkey looked round for help, but all deserted him. As he backed Hook advanced, and now the red spark was in his eye. With a despairing scream the pirate leapt upon Long Tom and precipitated himself into the sea.

"Four," said Slightly.

J M Barrie

Peter Pan (the motion picture event)

Then the sound! This time high up in the mast.

"Cap'n! It flies," said Smee.

Hook paled. "It is not possible."

Another pirate pointed to a shadow in the sails. "The brute has wings!" he howled fearfully.

Hook lifted his eyes. He saw it, too. The silhouette of a large figure was framed by the main sail.

Hook cursed. "And all this time it was a dragon. Into the rigging with ye! Hunt it down!"

"No, Cap'n, no!" Smee cried. He was terrified of dragons.

Hook shook his claw under Smee's nose. "Into the rigging or I'll cast anchor in you!"

Up the rigging climbed the pirates, while Hook aimed his pistol into the sails where the strange shadow still moved.

Suddenly there was a scream. A pirate dropped from the rigging and plunged headfirst into the dark water.

"What was that?" gasped Hook.

"One," said Slightly.

Clinging to the mast with one hand, Smee drew his pistol as a shadow glided across the highest sail. He pulled the trigger. The gun went off in a blast of fire and smoke and another pirate plunged into the sea.

"Two," said Slightly.

A scream rang out. A pirate, arms flapping, hit the water head first.

"Three," said Slightly.

Pirate Bill Jukes closed in on the shadow. He raised his dagger to plunge it into the creature's heart. But at that moment the sail blew aside, just as Bill Jukes swung his blade. On the way down, the pirate saw the creature they had been battling.

It was Tinker Bell, holding a clock and flitting among the masts. Her fairy glow had created the stranged shapes silhouetted by the sail.

"Four," said Slightly as Jukes slammed to the deck at Captain Hook's feet. The pirate whirled about and saw Peter Pan standing behind him, Wendy in his arms!

"So, Pan. This is all your doing," Hook snarled.

Peter Pan nodded and drew his sword. "Aye James Hook, it is all my doing."

Hook raised his own blade.

"Proud and insolent youth," cried Hook. "Prepare to meet thy doom."

Peter frowned, his bluer-than-blue eyes burning with determination.

"Dark and sinister man, have at thee!" yelled Peter.

With a crash of metal and a flash of sparks, their blades met.

It was Hook or Peter now!

Based on Peter Pan *by J M Barrie*

The Witches

"AND ALL US VITCHES SHOUT HOORAY!"

I hope you haven't forgotten that while all this was going on I was still stuck behind the screen on my hands and knees with one eye glued to the crack. I don't know how long I had been there but it seemed like forever. The worst part of it was not being allowed to cough or make a sound, and knowing that if I did, I was as good as dead. And all the way through, I was living in constant terror that one of the witches in the back row was going to get a whiff of my presence through those special nose-holes of hers.

My only hope, as I saw it, was the fact that I hadn't washed for days. That and the never-ending excitement and clapping and shouting that was going on in the room. The witches were thinking of nothing except The Grand High Witch up there on the platform and her great plan for wiping out all the children of England. They certainly weren't sniffing around for a child in the room. In their wildest dreams (if witches have dreams), that would never have occurred to any of them. I kept still and prayed.

The Grand High Witch's dreadful gloating song was over now, and the audience was clapping madly and shouting, "Brilliant! Sensational! Marvellous! You are a genius, O Brainy One! It is a thrilling invention, this Delayed Action Mouse-Maker! It is a winner! And the beauty of it is that the teachers will be the ones who bump off the stinking little children! It won't be us doing it! We shall never be caught!"

"Vitches are never caught!" snapped The Grand High Witch. "Attention now! I vont everybody's attention for I am about to be telling you vot you must do to prepare Formula 86 Delayed Action Mouse-Maker!"

Suddenly there came a great gasp from the audience. This was followed by a hubbub of shrieking and yelling, and I saw many of the witches leaping to their feet and pointing at the platform and crying out, "Mice! Mice! Mice! She's done it to show us! The Brainy One has turned two children into mice and there they are!"

I looked toward the platform. The mice were there all right, two of them, running around near The Grand High Witch's skirts.

But these were not field mice or house mice or wood mice or harvest mice. They were *white mice*! I recognised them immediately as being my own little William and Mary!

"Mice!" shouted the audience. "Our leader has made mice to appear out of nowhere! Get the mouse-traps! Fetch the cheese!"

I saw The Grand High Witch peering down at the floor and staring with obvious puzzlement at William and Mary. She bent lower to get a closer look. Then she straightened up and shouted, "Qviet!"

The audience became silent and sat down.

"These mice are nothing to do with me!" she shouted. "These mice are *pet* mice! These mice are qvite obviously belonging to some rrreepellent little child in the hotel! A boy it vill be for a certainty because girls are not keeping pet mice!"

"A boy!" cried the witches. "A filthy smelly little boy!"

Roald Dahl

The Witches: Plays for Children

And all us vitches shout

ALL: *[Standing]* Hooray!
[They rise to a big finish]

Down vith children! Do them in!
Boil their bones and fry their skin!
Bish them, sqvish them, bash them, mash them!
Brrreak them, shake them, slash them, smash them!
[The WITCHES cheer wildly. They sit again as the GRAND HIGH WITCH acknowledges their appreciation]
[Suddenly WITCH 1 leaps up and points to the back of the platform]

WITCH 1: Look! Look! Mice!
[Two white mice are progressing from one side to the other. They stop nervously, looking about]

BOY: *[Seeing them from behind the table]* Oh no! William and Mary!

WITCH 1: Our leader has done it to show us! The Brainy One has turned two children into mice!
[The GRAND HIGH WITCH has seen the mice. The other WITCHES start to applaud]

GRAND HIGH WITCH: Qviet
[She approaches the mice, who stop moving]

These mice are nothing to do with me. These mice are *pet* mice, qvite obviously belonging to some rrreepellent little child in this hotel.
[She chases the mice, stamping her feet]
[The mice scurry away and disappear]

WITCH 1: *[Menacingly]* A child! A filthy child. We'll sniff him out.
[The WITCHES start sniffing and some move ominously towards the table. BOY stiffens]
[Then, in the nick of time, there is a knock at the door. The WITCHES react, turning away from the table]

BRUNO: *[Outside the door]* Hey! Let me in!
[More knocks]

GRAND HIGH WITCH: Qvick, vitches, Vigs on!
[The WITCHES hurry to make themselves respectable]

BRUNO: *[Outside the door]* Hurry up! Twenty-five past three you said.

GRAND HIGH WITCH: Vitches. Vatch this demonstrrration. Earlier today I am giving a chocolate bar vith formula added to a smelly boy.

BRUNO: *[Outside the door]* Where's them chocolate bars you promised? I'm here to collect! Dish 'em out!

GRAND HIGH WITCH: Not only smelly but grrreedy. The formula is timed for half-past three.
[She puts on her wig, handed to her by WITCH 1, but not her face mask]

Let him in.
[WITCH 1 takes the key and exits upstage to unlock the door]
[BRUNO enters and approaches. WITCH 1 follows him in]
[The GRAND HIGH WITCH, keeping her back towards him, comes downstage, off the platform]

[Soft and gentle] Darling little man. I haf your chocolate all rrready for you. Do come and say hello to all these lovely ladies.
[BRUNO descends the platform, eyed eagerly by the WITCHES]

BRUNO: OK, where's my chocolate? Six bars you said.

GRAND HIGH WITCH: *[Checking her watch]* Thirty seconds to go.

BRUNO: What?
[He receives no reply. He approaches the GRAND HIGH WITCH]
What the heck's going on?

GRAND HIGH WITCH: Twenty seconds!

BRUNO: *[Getting suspicious]* Gimme the chocolate and let me get out of here.

GRAND HIGH WITCH: Fifteen seconds!

BRUNO: *[Looking at the WITCHES]* Will one of you crazy punks kindly tell me what all this is about?

GRAND HIGH WITCH: Ten seconds!
[She turns her face to BRUNO, who reacts with a terrified scream]

WITCHES: *[Surrounding BRUNO menacingly, but also in delighted anticipation]* Nine... eight... seven... six... five... four... three... two... one... zero!

GRAND HIGH WITCH: Vee haf ignition.

Roald Dahl and David Wood

The Story of Tracy Beaker

"Oh, I get it," I said in this jokey silly voice, "So they're going to give the boring old baby away because they can't cope with it. And keep me. Because they had me first, didn't they?"

"Tracy–"

"They're not really going to dump me, are they?"

"They still very much want to keep in touch with you and – "

"So why can't I go on living with them? Look, I'll help all I can. Julie doesn't need to worry. I'll be just like a second mum to this baby. I know all what to do. I can give it its bottle and change its soggy nappy and thump it on its back to bring up its wind. I'm dead experienced where babies are concerned."

"Yes, I know, Tracy. But that's the trouble. You see, when Julie and Ted first fostered you, we did tell them a bit about your background, and the trouble you had in your first foster home. You know, when you shut the baby up in the cupboard – "

"That was Steve. And he wasn't a baby. He was a foul little toddler, and he kept mucking up our bedroom so I tidied him up into the cupboard just for a bit so I could get everything straightened out."

"And there was the ghost game that got totally out of hand – "

"Oh that! All those little kids *loved* that game. I was ever so good at finding the right hiding places and then I'd start an eerie sort of moan and then I'd jump out at them, wearing this old white sheet."

"And everyone got scared silly."

"No they didn't. They just squealed because they were excited. *I* was the one who should have been scared, because they were all ghost-busters, you see and I was the poor little ghost and –"

"OK, OK, but the point is, Tracy, it makes it plain in your records that you don't always get on well with little children."

"That's a whopping great lie! What about Camilla? I looked after her at the children's home and she loved me, she really did."

"Yes, I'm sure that's true Tracy, but – Well, the thing is, Julie and Ted still feel they don't want to take any chances. They're worried you might feel a bit uncomfortable with a baby in the house."

"So they're pushing me out?"

"But like I said, they still want to keep in touch with you and maybe take you out for tea sometimes."

"No way," I said. "I don't want to see them ever again."

"Oh Tracy, that's silly. That's just cutting off your own nose to spite your face," said Elaine. That's such a daft expression. How on earth would you go about it?

It wouldn't half hurt.

It hurt a lot leaving Julie and Ted's.

Jacqueline Wilson

My Friend Walter

My name is Elizabeth Throckmorton and I'll be eleven on my next birthday. Aunty Ellie (you'll meet her later) calls me her "china doll" on account of my pale skin and straight black hair. I'm small for my age, so people at school think I'm feeble and fragile which I'm not. I don't talk much, so they think I'm unfriendly which I'm not. I just get on better with myself than anyone else that's all.

Around me at home there's my family. First there's Father, who's a farmer. Father treats me like a boy. I think he always wanted me to be a boy, really. Then there's Mother, who's always busy. If she's not out on the farm she's scurrying about the house with a broom or a pile of dirty washing. She never stops. She doesn't seem to have time to talk to me much these days, not since little Jim was born; but we understand each other – always have done. Not like my big brother Will. We haven't got much in common, Will and me. When he's not shooting or fishing, he's down in the cellar making horrible smells in the chemistry laboratory he's set up down there. I'd like to like him more – I know I ought to.

Then there's Little Jim. Little Jim was born about eight months ago. He always needs feeding or changing or picking up or mopping up. I spend a lot of time looking after Little Jim, but he doesn't seem to appreciate it. He loves to pull my hair out by the roots or to tear my ears off whenever he can. He never does that to Gran. Gran has been living with us in the house as long as I can remember. She's nearly eighty now. I know she means well, but she does go on a bit sometimes.

I suppose you could say that it was an ordinary sort of morning in our house the day the postcard came. The toast burnt and Father shouted and spluttered with his mouth full of cornflakes. I was giving Little Jim his breakfast. Mother was trying to rescue the toast and see to Gran's boiled egg, all at the same time. Will was in the bathroom. He's always down last. Humph is our black and white sheepdog with a killer instinct for letters and postcards, and it was Humph that heard the postman first. He rose with a terrible growl from his catching position under Little Jim's high chair and fairly flew out of the kitchen door. He returned seconds later his tail high with triumph, a postcard in his mouth, wet and punctured as usual. Mother told him to drop it. Humph looked at her blankly, pretending not to understand. He had learned that if you hold out long enough you get one of Little Jim's rusks in exchange for the post. And sure enough he got one this morning.

"Well, I'm blowed," Father said, picking the postcard off the floor. "What do you make of this, then?"

"Of what, dear?" said Mother, wiping her hands on her apron and coming to look over his shoulder.

"Can't hardly make it out," said Father, peering at it closely. "'S funny writing, don't you think? Anyway, seems we're all invited to some sort of family reunion. Never heard of such a thing, have you?"

Michael Morpurgo

Mrs Frisby and the Rats of Nimh

Mrs Frisby spelled it out slowly: The Plan of the Rats of Nimh. What, or where was Nimh? The name had a strange and far-away sound. Had these rats, then, come here from somewhere else? Did that explain why they had books and electric lights and wires and an electric motor? Yet they had been here – or at least there had been rats here – for as long as she could remember. Still, that was not so very long.

She wondered what other things they had. Suddenly she had an almost overwhelming desire to look around – to see what was behind the open doors and down the other corridors. She went to the door, opened it, and looked out into the hall. It was entirely deserted and silent, except that when she listened carefully she could hear a faint humming in the distance, as if something were running – another motor?

She started out into the hall, and then changed her mind. Better not. Nicodemus had been friendly – they had all been friendly – but explicit. He had said she was to wait in the library. And she was not there to pry but to get help. She went back into the library, closed the door, and sat on one of the benches. The books on the table were mostly paperbacks – small enough so that the rats could handle them easily enough, but too big for her; so she sat in front of the blackboard and looked at it again.

Beneath the title across the top, in neatly chalked handwriting, were columns of words and figures:

Schedule

January:
Group 1 (10):	Oats.	30 loads = 2 bu.
Group 2 (10):	Wheat.	30 loads = 2 bu.
Group 3 (10):	Corn.	20 loads = 1½ bu.
Group 4 (10):	Misc. seeds	Est. 10 loads total

The rest of the blackboard was filled with more rows of figures, each headed by the name of a month: February, March, April, May, and so on until the end of July. At the bottom a separate square was ruled off:

Ploughs (Arthur's group) (14)
Plough No. 2. Complete: Jan. 1
Plough No. 3. Complete: Feb. 10
Plough No. 4. Complete: Mar. 20

Mrs Frisby stared at all this trying to make head or tail of it, but she could not. It was quite incomprehensible. She was still puzzling over it when the door opened and a rat came in. It was a girl-rat, small and quite young, judging by her looks. She was carrying a pencil and some papers and looking at the papers as she walked, so that she did not see Mrs Frisby at first. When she did she gasped and dropped the papers, scattering them on the floor. Her eyes opened wide.

"Who are you?" she asked. "I don't know you. How did you get in?" She backed towards the door.

"It's all right," said Mrs Frisby. "I'm a friend of Mr Ages." The rat was very young indeed, only a child.

"But why are you in here? Who let you in?"

"Nicodemus. He told me to wait here."

The girl-rat looked doubtful. "You might be a spy."

"A spy! How could I be? A spy from where?"

"I don't know. From outside. Maybe from Nimh?"

"I don't even know what Nimh is."

"That's what you *say*."

Robert O'Brien

When Hitler Stole Pink Rabbit

Afterwards Anna was very ashamed of her outburst. After all, she had really known all the time that Mama and Papa had no choice but to send her and Max away. All she had done was make everyone feel worse about something that had to happen anyway. Why couldn't she have kept quiet? She worried about it in bed and when she woke up early the next morning she felt she must do something. She still had her prize money left – she would go out and buy croissants for everybody's breakfast.

There was a little breeze blowing for the first time in weeks and when she came back from the bakers with the hot croissants in a bag she suddenly felt much happier. It would all work out somehow – everything would be all right.

A man was talking to the concierge in a strong German accent and as she passed Anna heard him asking for Papa.

"I'll take you up," she said, disregarding the concierge, and the concierge, in offended silence, handed her a letter. Anna looked down at it and saw with a sudden quickening of the pulse that it had an English stamp. All the way up in the lift she could think of nothing but what might be inside the letter, and she only remembered Papa's visitor when he spoke to her.

"You must be Anna," he said and she nodded.

He was a shabby-looking man with a sad voice.

"Papa!" cried Anna as they entered the flat. "I've brought some croissants for breakfast and there's a letter and someone to see you!"

"Someone here? Now?" said Papa as he emerged from his room, tying his tie.

He drew the visitor into the dining room and Anna followed with the letter in her hand.

"How do you do, Herr…?"

"Rosenfeld," said the man with a little bow. "I used to be an actor in Berlin but you don't know me. Only small parts you understand." He smiled, showing irregular yellow teeth and added with apparent irrelevance, "I have a nephew in the confectionery business."

"Papa…" said Anna, holding out the letter, but Papa said, "Later!"

Herr Rosenfeld seemed to find it difficult to say what he had come for. His sad eyes kept roaming round the dining room while he considered one opening after another and dismissed each one. At last he put his hand in his pocket and pulled out a small parcel wrapped in brown paper.

"I have brought you this," he said and handed it to Papa. Papa unwrapped it. It was a watch – an old silver watch – and there was something familiar about it.

"Julius!" cried Papa.

Herr Rosenfeld nodded sadly. "I am the bearer of bad news."

Onkel Julius was dead.

While Mama gave Herr Rosenfeld some coffee and he absent-mindedly nibbled one of Anna's croissants he told them how Onkel Julius had died. He had been dismissed from his post as curator of the Berlin Natural History Museum nearly a year ago.

"Surely you knew," said Herr Rosenfeld.

Judith Kerr

The Sheep-Pig (2)

"And the handler, he's not even said a word, not even moved, just stood there leaning on his stick."

"Ah, but he'll have to move now – you're never going to tell me that pig can shed four sheep out of the ten on his own!"

The Shedding Ring was in a circle perhaps forty yards in diameter, marked out by little heaps of sawdust, and into it the sheep walked, still calm, still collected, and stood waiting.

Outside the circle Babe waited, his eyes on Hogget.

The crowd waited.

Mrs Hogget waited.

Hundreds of thousands of viewers waited.

Then, just as it seemed nothing more would happen, that the man had somehow lost control of the sheep-pig, that the sheep-pig had lost interest in his sheep, Farmer Hogget raised his stick and with it gave one sharp tap upon the great sarsen-stone, a tap that sounded like a pistol-shot in the tense atmosphere.

And at this signal Babe walked gently into the circle and up to his sheep.

"Beautifully done," he said to them quietly. "I can't tell you how grateful I am to you all. Now, if the four ladies with the collars would kindly walk out of the ring when I give you a grunt, I should be so much obliged. Then if you would all be good enough to wait until my boss has walked across to the final collecting pen over there and opened its gate, all that remains for you to do is to pop in. Would you do that? Please?"

"A-a-a-a-a-a-a-ar," they said softly, and as Babe gave one deep grunt the four collared sheep detached themselves from their companions and calmly, unhurriedly, walked out of the Shedding Ring.

Unmoving, held by the magic of the moment, the crowd watched with no sound but a great sigh of amazement. No one could quite believe his eyes. No one seemed to notice that the wind had dropped and the rain had stopped. No one was surprised when a single shaft of sunshine came suddenly through a hole in the grey clouds and shone full upon the great sarsen-stone. Slowly, with his long strides, Hogget left it and walked to the little enclosure of hurdles, the final test of his shepherding. He opened its gate and stood, silent still, while the shed animals walked back into the ring to rejoin the rest.

Then he nodded once at Babe, no more, and steadily, smartly, straightly, the ten sheep, with the sheep-pig at their heels, marched into the final pen, and Hogget closed the gate.

As he dropped the loop of rope over the hurdle stake, everyone could see the judges' marks.

A hundred out of a hundred, the perfect performance, never before matched by man and dog in the whole history of sheep dog trials, but now achieved by man and pig, and everyone went mad!

Dick King-Smith

Jabberwocky

'Twas brillig, and the slithy toves
Did gyre and gimble in the wabe:
All mimsy were the borogoves,
And the mome raths outgrabe

"Beware the Jabberwock, my son!
The jaws that bite, the claws that catch!
Beware the Jubjub bird, and shun
The frumious Bandersnatch!"

He took his vorpal sword in hand:
Long time the manxome foe he sought –
So rested he by the Tumtum tree,
And stood awhile in thought.

And, as in uffish thought he stood,
The Jabberwock, the eyes of flame,
Came whiffling through the tulgey wood,
And burbled as it came!

One, two! One, two! And through and through
The vorpal blade went snicker-snack!
He left it dead, and with its head
He went galumphing back.

"And hast thou slain the Jabberwock?
Come to my arms, my beamish boy!
O frabjous day! Callooh! Callay!"
He chortled in his joy

'Twas brillig, and the slithy toves
Did gyre and gimble in the wabe:
All mimsy were the borogoves,
And the mome raths outgrabe.

Lewis Carroll

The Witches' Chant

"Down with the children! Do them in!
Boil their bones and fry their skin!
Bish them, sqvish them, bash them, mash them!
Brrreak them, shake them, slash them, smash them!
Offer them chocs with magic powder!
Say 'Eat up!' then say it louder.
Crrram them full of sticky eats,
Send them home still guzzling sveets.
And in the morning little fools
Go marching off to separate schools.
A girl feels sick and goes all pale.
She yells, 'Hey look! I've grrrown a tail!'
A boy who's standing next to her
Screams, 'Help! I think I'm grrrowing fur!'
Another shouts, 'Vee look like frrreaks!
There's viskers growing on our cheeks!'
A boy who vos extremely tall
Cries out, 'Vot's wrong? I'm grrrowing small!'
Four tiny legs begin to sprrrout
From everybody rrround about.
And all at vunce, all in a trrrice,
There are no children! Only MICE!

In every school is mice galore
All rrrunning rrround the school-rrroom floor!
And all the poor demented teachers
Is yelling, 'Hey, who are these crrreatures?'
They stand upon the desks and shout,
'Get out, you filthy mice! Get out!
Vill somone fetch some mouse-trrraps, please!
And don't forrrget to bring the cheese!'
Now mouse-trrraps come and every trrrap
Goes *snippy-snip* and *snappy-snap*.
The mouse-trrraps have a powerful spring,
The springs go *crack* and *snap* and *ping*!
Is lovely noise for us to hear!
Is music to a vitch's ear!
Dead mice is every place arrround,
Piled two feet deep upon the grrround,
Vith teachers searching left and rrright,
But not a single child in sight!
The teachers cry, 'Vot's going on?
Oh vhere have all the children gone?
Is half-past nine and as a rrrule
They're never late as this for school!'
Poor teachers don't know vot to do.
Some sit and rrread, and just a few
Amuse themselves throughout the day
By sweeping all the mice avay.
AND ALL US VITCHES SHOUT HOORAY!"

Roald Dahl

Fire, Burn; and Cauldron, Bubble

Round about the cauldron go:
In the poisoned entrails throw.
Toad, that under cold stone
Days and nights has thirty-one
Sweltered venom sleeping got,
Boil thou first i'th' charmed pot!

Double, double toil and trouble;
Fire, burn; and cauldron, bubble.

Fillet of a fenny snake,
In the cauldron boil and bake:
Eye of newt and toe of frog,
Wool of bat and tongue of dog,
Adder's fork and blind-worm's sting,
Lizard's leg and howlet's wing,
For a charm of powerful trouble,
Like a hell-broth boil and bubble.

Double, double toil and trouble;
Fire, burn; and cauldron, bubble.

William Shakespeare

Charlotte Sometimes (1)

Next morning Charlotte woke before the bell. At least no bell had woken her and she doubted if she would have slept through it on only the second day of term. As she floated out of sleep she remembered it was Sunday so that the bell would be rung quite late in any case.

She lay with her eyes shut for a while, comfortable as a cat, the sun warm and rosy on her lids. When at last she opened them she found she was looking almost into the sun itself, though its dazzle was broken by a tree. In return it blurred the dark limits of the tree's branches, beamed through them in places and shone full into her eyes, making her blink.

The tree; Charlotte sat up with a jump. For there should be no tree in the sun's way. In fact you would not expect to see the sun at all because the new building should have hidden it.

But though there had been a building there yesterday and no tree, today there was a tree and no building. The tree was a huge, dark cedar tree.

Charlotte shot back down the bed, hiding her head beneath the covers. It must be a dream. If she counted ten before looking out again she would find she had imagined it. As a little girl she'd often lain like that under the bedclothes, counting, but hoping to open her eyes on a different world – a palace perhaps, herself a princess – whereas now she merely wanted things the same as yesterday, the red brick building, the shadowed room; no sun, no tree. Having counted to a hundred just to make sure, she peered out again to find the sun still there with its coloured, dusty beams; also the cedar tree.

Slowly, reluctantly, she turned her head to look at the room itself. Her sun-dazzled eyes could tell scarcely more at first than its shape and colour, both still apparently the same. She could see black iron bedsteads too, four of them, but as her sight cleared saw that against the wall opposite where the fifth bed should have been, was a huge white painted cupboard with drawers underneath. All the proper chest-of-drawers had gone, and their photographs and ornaments, their dogs and cats and gnomes, their calendars and combs and hairbrushes; so had the curtained cubicle and the wash basin with its shining taps. In place of that a white enamel basin stood on a stand, a white enamel jug beside it. On the chair beside Charlotte's bed instead of her new book there lay a little prayer-book in a floppy leather cover and a rather shabby bible with gold-edged pages.

Janet and Vanessa must have got up early, Charlotte thought wildly, for two of the beds were empty, their coverings smooth as if not slept in at all. They must have made their beds and gone out so quietly that no one had woken.

But that did not explain why the cupboard stood where Elizabeth's bed should have been, nor why the hair on Susannah's pillow next to her own was no longer dark like Susannah's hair, but a lightish brown.

The hump beneath the blankets stirred. There was a little groaning and sighing and a hand reached out, curling itself and uncurling again, terrifying Charlotte, because if she did not know who the hand belonged to and the light brown hair, how would that person know who Charlotte was, and however was she to explain her presence there?

The hump spoke. "Clare," it said crossly. "*Clare.*"

Charlotte looked wildly about but found no one to answer, except herself.

Penelope Farmer

Charlotte Sometimes (2)

"*Clare*, are you awake?" demanded the hump, more crossly than ever.

"I'm awake," Charlotte said, which was true, without her having to admit she was not Clare, whoever Clare might be.

"Well then, why didn't you say so before?"

"I..." began Charlotte. "Because I..." And then to her horror the girl in the other bed sat up abruptly. She was quite a little girl, much smaller than Susannah, indeed she looked smaller than anyone Charlotte had seen so far at boarding school, though she wore the regulation nightdress. She had long hair and a round face, puzzled rather than cross and red and creased looking on the side nearest Charlotte on which she must have been lying.

She looked at Charlotte as if she saw just whom she expected to see and said, "Is it early Clare? Has the bell gone? Have we got to get up?"

"But I'm not Clare," Charlotte began to say hopelessly, then stopped herself, explanation being impossible, especially since this girl seemed to think so incredibly that she was Clare.

"What's the matter with you, Clare?" the little girl cried. "Why don't you answer me? Is it time to get up? Is it, is it, *is* it?"

"I haven't heard a bell yet," Charlotte said.

"Oh, well, then it can't be time to get up. We mustn't be late. Aunt Dolly said we'd get into fearful trouble if we were late for breakfast at school."

Charlotte was scarcely listening, thinking, horrified that perhaps she was not Charlotte any more but had changed into someone else. That would explain why the little girl had greeted her as Clare.

She held out her hands to see. They did not look any different, but she wondered suddenly if she knew them well enough to tell. They were quite ordinary hands, having fingers of medium length and no scars or marks to distinguish them. With her hands she stroked her hair, which was quite straight and fell some way below her shoulders just as it had done the day before. When she picked up a piece and drew it round, it seemed the same colour too, fairish, nondescript. She moved her hands rapidly over all her face, eyes, mouth, chin, cheeks, nose, and then again, more slowly. But it did not tell her very much. Could you just by feel, she wondered, recognize your own face? A blind person might, whose touch was sight, but she was not sure she could trust herself to do it. Her mouth seemed wider than she'd thought, her nose felt narrower.

"What are you feeling your face for like that?" the little girl asked curiously.

"Oh... oh... nothing in particular..." And at that moment, luckily, the bell went, an old fashioned clanging bell, not the shrill electric one of the night before. Charlotte jumped out of bed immediately, but the other huddled back into hers, saying, "I don't feel like getting up, but of course you do what we ought, Clare, you always do."

Charlotte was by now so desperate she did not care if the girl found her odd. She ran to the only mirror in the room, a square, rather stained and pitted one hung just beside the door, and the relief that came when she saw her own face staring back at her was huger than she could have thought.

Except, if she was Charlotte, why did the little girl take her for somebody else called Clare? Just then the door opened and a woman came in, a tall, thin woman with her hair screwed up on her head under a white cap like a nurse's cap, her head very small like the knob on a knitting needle. Her big white apron was starched to shine, indeed she shone all over as if newly polished: shoes, hair, apron, even her nose. Her skirt, Charlotte noticed, was so long it stopped not far above her ankles.

Penelope Farmer

The Borrowers

"Nowadays, I suppose," Mrs May went on slowly, "if they exist at all, you only find them in houses which are old and quiet and deep in the country – and where the human beings live to a routine. Routine is their safeguard: it is important for them to know which rooms are used and when. They do not stay long where there are careless people, unruly children or certain household pets.

"This particular old house, of course, was ideal – although as far as some of them were concerned, a trifle cold and empty. Great Aunt Sophy was bedridden, through a hunting accident some twenty years before, and as for other human beings there was only Mrs Driver the cook, Crampfurl the gardener, and, at rare intervals, an odd housemaid or such. My brother, too, when he went there after rheumatic fever, had to spend long hours in bed, and for those first weeks it seems the Borrowers did not know of his existence.

"He slept in the old night-nursery, beyond the schoolroom. The schoolroom, at that time, was sheeted and shrouded and filled with junk – odd trunks, a broken sewing machine, a desk, a dressmaker's dummy, a table, some chairs, and a disused pianola – as the children who had used it, Great Aunt Sophy's children, had long since grown up, married, died, or gone away. The night-nursery opened out of the schoolroom and, from his bed, my brother could see the oil painting of the battle of Waterloo which hung above the schoolroom fireplace and, on the wall, a corner cupboard with glass doors in which was set out, on hooks and shelves, a doll's tea service – very delicate and old. At night, if the schoolroom door was open, he had a view down the lighted passage which led to the staircase, and it would comfort him to see, each evening at dusk, Mrs Driver appear at the head of the stairs and cross the passage carrying a tray for Aunt Sophy with Bath Oliver biscuits and the tall, cut-glass decanter of Fine Old Pale Madeira. On her way out Mrs Driver would pause and lower the gas jet in the passage to a dim, blue flame, and then he would watch her as she stumped away downstairs, sinking slowly out of sight between the banisters.

"Under this passage, in the hall below, there was a clock, and through the night he would hear it strike the hours. It was a grandfather clock and very old. Mr Frith of Leighton Buzzard came each month to wind it, as his father had come before him and his great uncle before that. For eighty years, they said (and to Mr Frith's knowledge), it had not stopped and, as far as anyone could tell, for as many years before that. The great thing was – that it must never be moved. It stood against the wainscot, and the stone flags around it had been washed so often that a little platform, my brother said, rose up inside.

"And under this clock, below the wainscot, there was a hole…"

Mary Norton

Alice Through the Looking Glass

"And as for *you*," she went on, turning fiercely upon the Red Queen, whom she considered as the cause of all the mischief – but the Queen was no longer at her side – she had suddenly dwindled down to the size of a little doll, and was now on the table, merrily running round and round after her own shawl, which was trailing behind her.

At any other time, Alice would have felt surprised at this, but she was far too excited to be surprised at anything *now*. "As for *you*," she repeated, catching hold of the little creature in the very act of jumping over a bottle which had just lighted upon the table, "I'll shake you into a kitten, that I will!"

Chapter 10 SHAKING

She took her off the table as she spoke, and shook her backwards and forwards with all her might.

The Red Queen made no resistance whatever; only her face grew very small, and her eyes got large and green: and still, as Alice went on shaking her, she kept growing shorter – and fatter – and softer – and rounder – and –

Chapter 11 WAKING

– and it really *was* a kitten, after all.

Chapter 12 WHICH DREAMED IT?

"Your Red Majesty shouldn't purr so loud," Alice said, rubbing her eyes, and addressing the kitten, respectfully, yet with some severity. "You woke me out of oh! such a nice dream! And you've been along with me, Kitty – all through the Looking-Glass world. Did you know it, dear?"

It is a very inconvenient habit of kittens (Alice had once made the remark) that, whatever you say to them, they *always* purr. "If they would only purr for 'yes', and mew for 'no', or any rule of that sort," she had said, "so that one could keep up a conversation! But how *can* you talk with a person if they always say the same thing?"

On this occasion the kitten only purred: and it was impossible to guess whether it meant "yes" or "no".

So Alice hunted among the chessmen on the table until she found the Red Queen: then she went down on her knees on the hearth-rug, and put the kitten and the Queen to look at each other. "Now, Kitty!" she cried, clapping her hands triumphantly. "Confess that was what you turned into!"

"And what did *Dinah* turn to, I wonder?" she prattled on, as she settled comfortably down, with one elbow on the rug, and her chin in her hand, to watch the kittens. "Tell me, Dinah, did you turn to Humpty Dumpty? I *think* you did – however, you'd better not mention it to your friends just yet, for I'm not sure.

"By the way, Kitty, if only you'd been really with me in my dream, there was one thing you *would* have enjoyed – I had such a quantity of poetry said to me, all about fishes! Tomorrow morning you shall have a real treat. All the time you're eating your breakfast, I'll repeat 'The Walrus and the Carpenter' to you; and then you can make believe it's oysters, dear!

"Now, Kitty, let's consider who it was that dreamed it all. This is a serious question, my dear, and you should *not* go on licking your paw like that – as if Dinah hadn't washed you this morning! You see, Kitty, it *must* have been either me or the Red King. He was part of my dream, of course – but then I was part of his dream too! *Was* it the Red King, Kitty? You were his wife, my dear, so you ought to know – Oh, Kitty, *do* help settle it! I'm sure your paw can wait!" But the provoking kitten only began on the other paw, and pretended he hadn't heard the question.

Which do *you* think it was?

Lewis Carroll

The Story of Zoe

"Get this lot cleared up, girl!"

Zoe was already exhausted, and now she had more mess to cope with: a floor littered with chocolate bar wrappers, crisp packets and empty drink cans. They were the remains of her stepsisters' most recent snack. She, of course, had been offered none of it.

As Zoe swept and mopped, her overweight stepsisters sprawled in front of the television, pausing occasionally to unwrap a sweet or grab a handful of nuts.

"When you've finished doing that, get the washing ironed," snarled Zoe's stepmother. "I want my two little girls to look their prettiest for tonight's disco," she added, smiling fondly at her two daughters.

The evening's disco was a special one: it was an annual event, held in the Civic Hall, as a leaving celebration for Year 6 students at the two local schools. Absolutely everyone went… except Zoe. She had no money for a ticket, and she had nothing to wear.

That evening, her two stepsisters got ready.

"I'm wearing my special hair extensions," bragged one.

"I love my lurex leggings," squealed the other.

They cackled away, each sure that she looked spectacular. Zoe, whose job was to pass them everything they demanded, thought they both looked hideous: their clothes were too glittery, too tight, too tasteless.

The two sisters and their mother set off for the Civic Hall, leaving Zoe with yet more work to do. As she leaned on her brush, there was a sudden ring at the door. Cautiously, she opened it. Before she had time to even open her mouth, the strange little woman standing in front of her began to speak.

"I am the area children's watchdog. I have observed that your treatment is unfair: you should and MUST go to the dance. Here is your ticket and outfit, but everything must be returned by 10 p.m. Get changed quickly, and wait here for your limousine. Remember – 10 p.m."

Zoe blinked, and the woman had gone. This was unbelievable! She rummaged through the bag, found the most fabulous outfit – even jewellery. In a daze, she got ready, and five minutes later a chauffeur-driven limousine pulled up at the door.

The evening was fantastic. There was music from a local group who had already appeared on TV, a buffet supper, and, best of all, Mark. She had always liked Mark, but from afar. All the girls liked Mark: he was clever, good at everything, liked a laugh, and was handsome. He was also a great dancer. Zoe's stepsisters kept parading themselves in front of him and asking him to dance with them, but he would have nothing to do with them. He spent all evening talking to and dancing with a girl he thought he had never seen before. The girl was the transformed Zoe.

At two minutes to ten, Zoe suddenly became aware of the time. She blurted out a farewell, and made a dash for her waiting limousine. As she ran, the clasp on her choker came loose, and slipped to the ground. Mark, who raced out of the hall after her, could find no trace of her – no trace, except the choker on the ground. He picked it up. Now he had a way to find her.

What Katy Did (1)

A constant feud raged between the two schools as to the respective merits of the teachers and the instruction. The Knight girls, for some unknown reason, considered themselves genteel and the Miller girls vulgar, and took no pains to conceal this opinion; while the Miller girls, on the other hand, retaliated by being as aggravating as they knew how. They spent their recesses and intermissions mostly in making faces through the knot-holes in the fence, and over the top of it, when they could get there, which wasn't an easy thing to do, as the fence was pretty high. The Knight girls could make faces too, for all their gentility. Their yard had one great advantage over the other: it possessed a wood-shed, with a climbable roof, which commanded Miss Miller's premises, and upon this the girls used to sit in rows, turning their noses up at the next yard, and irritating the foe by jeering remarks. "Knights" and "Millerites" the two schools called each other; and the feud raged so high that sometimes it was hardly safe for a Knight to meet a Millerite in the street; all of which, as may be imagined, was exceedingly improving both to the manners and morals of the young ladies concerned.

One morning, not long after the day in Paradise, Katy was late. She could not find her things. Her algebra, as she expressed it, had "gone and lost itself", her slate was missing, and the string was off her sun-bonnet. She ran about, searching for these articles and banging doors, till Aunt Izzie was out of patience.

"As for your algebra," she said, "if it is that very dirty book with only one cover, and scribbled all over the leaves, you will find it under the kitchen table. Philly was playing before breakfast that it was a pig; no wonder, I'm sure, for it looks good for nothing else. How you do manage to spoil your school-books in this manner, Katy, I cannot imagine. It is less than a month since your father got you a new algebra, and look at it now – not fit to be carried about. I do wish you'd realise what books cost!

"About your slate," she went on, "I know nothing; but here is the bonnet string;" taking it out of her pocket.

"Oh, thank you!" said Katy, hastily sticking it on with a pin.

"Katy Carr!" almost screamed Miss Izzie, "what *are* you about? Pinning on your bonnet string! Mercy on me! what shiftless thing will you do next? Now stand still and don't fidget! You shan't stir till I have sewed it on properly."

It wasn't easy to "stand still and not fidget", with Aunt Izzie fussing away and lecturing, and now and then, in a moment of forgetfulness, sticking her needle into one's chin. Katy bore it as well as she could, only shifting perpetually from one foot to the other, and now and then uttering a little snort, like an impatient horse. The minute she was released she flew into the kitchen, seized the algebra, and rushed like a whirlwind to the gate, where good little Clover stood patiently waiting, though all ready herself, and terribly afraid she should be late.

"We shall have to run," gasped Katy, quite out of breath. "Aunt Izzie kept me. She has been so horrid!"

They did run as fast as they could, but time ran faster. And before they were half-way to school the town clock struck nine, and all the hope was over. This vexed Katy very much; for, though often late, she was always eager to be early.

"There," she said, stopping short, "I shall just tell Aunt Izzie that it was her fault. It is *too* bad." And she marched into the school in a very cross mood.

A day begun in this manner is pretty sure to end badly, as most of us know.

Susan Coolidge

Five Children and It (1)

"What?"

"It said, 'You let me alone.'"

But Cyril merely observed that his sister must have gone off her nut, and he and Robert dug with spades while Anthea sat on the edge of the hole, jumping up and down with hotness and anxiety. They dug carefully, and presently everyone could see that there really was something moving in the bottom of the Australian hole.

Then Anthea cried out, "*I'm* not afraid. Let me dig," and fell on her knees and began to scratch like a dog does when he has suddenly remembered where it was he buried his bone.

"Oh, I felt fur," she cried, half laughing and half crying. "I did indeed! I did!" when suddenly a dry husky voice in the sand made them all jump back, and their hearts jumped nearly as fast as they did.

"Let me alone," it said. And now everyone heard the voice and looked at the others to see if they had too.

"But we want to see you," said Robert bravely.

"I wish you'd come out," said Anthea, also taking courage.

"Oh, well – if that's your wish," the voice said, and the sand stirred and spun and scattered, and something brown and furry and fat came rolling into the hole and the sand fell off it, and it sat there yawning and rubbing the ends of its eyes with its hands.

"I believe I must have dropped asleep," it said, stretching itself.

The children stood around the hole in a ring, looking at the creature they had found. It was worth looking at. Its eyes were on long horns like a snail's eyes, and it could move them in and out like telescopes; it had ears like a bat's ears, and its tubby body was shaped like a spider's and covered in thick soft fur; its legs and arms were furry too, and it had hands and feet like a monkey's.

"What on earth is it?" Jane said. "Shall we take it home?"

The thing turned its long eyes to look at her, and said: "Does she always talk nonsense, or is it only the rubbish on her head that makes her so silly?"

It looked scornfully at Jane's hat as it spoke.

"She doesn't mean to be silly," Anthea said gently; "we none of us do, whatever you may think! Don't be frightened; we don't want to hurt you, you know."

"Hurt *me*!" it said. "*Me* frightened? Upon my word! Why, you talk as if I were nobody in particular." All its fur stood out like a cat's when it is going to fight.

"Well," said Anthea, still kindly, "perhaps if we knew who you are in particular we could think of something to say that wouldn't make you cross. Everything we've said so far seems to have. Who are you? And don't get angry! Because we really don't know."

"You don't know?" it said. "Well I knew the world had changed – but – well, really – do you mean to tell me seriously that you don't know a Psammead when you see one?"

"A Sammyadd? That's Greek to me,"

"So it is to everyone," said the creature sharply. "Well, in plain English, then, a *Sand-fairy*. Don't you know a Sand-fairy when you see one?"

It looked so grieved and hurt that Jane hastened to say, "Of course I see you are, *now*. It's quite plain now one comes to look at you."

"You came to look at me, several sentences ago," it said crossly, beginning to curl up again in the sand.

"Oh – don't go away again! Do talk some more," Robert cried. "I didn't know you were a Sand-fairy, but I knew directly I saw you that you were much the wonderfullest thing I'd ever seen."

The Sand-fairy seemed a shade less disagreeable after this.

"It isn't talking I mind," it said, "as long as you're reasonably civil. But I'm not going to make polite conversation for you. If you talk nicely to me, perhaps I'll answer you, and perhaps I won't. Now say something."

Of course no one could think of anything to say, but at last Robert thought of "How long have you lived here?" and he said it at once.

"Oh, ages – several thousand years," replied the Psammead.

"Tell us about it. Do."

"It's all in books."

"*You* aren't!" Jane said. "Oh, tell us everything you can about yourself! We don't know anything about you, and you *are* so nice."

The Sand-fairy smoothed his long rat-like whiskers and smiled between them.

...

It drew its eyes in and said:

"How very sunny it is – quite like the old times. Where do you get your Megatheriums from now?"

"What?" said the children all at once. It is difficult always to remember that "what" is not polite, especially in moments of surprise or agitation.

"Are Pterodactyls plentiful now?" the Sand-fairy went on.

The children were unable to reply.

E Nesbit

Shadow of the Minotaur (1)

… he found himself at a junction in the maze. Then, as he looked around, his heart lurched. He had just tripped over the thread that marked his own path. The string lay criss-crossed over itself.

"I'm going round in circles," he said in dismay, and his voice rebounded in the chill tunnels. He peered into each of the passageways that led off from the junction. Ignoring the one where the thread lay accusingly on the floor, he made his way down a second tunnel. This one sloped gradually downward.

It was getting colder and the stone floor was oily with puddles of foul water. Dimly shining globs of something unspeakable floated on their dull surfaces. Touching the walls earlier had turned his stomach. He had no intention of making the same mistake with the floor.

Something stirred. A rat? He had never dreamed that he would ever wish for a rat, but then he would have taken a hundred of the things, rather than the lumbering form waiting for him in the darkness. Hooves scraped on the floor. The sound was made by something big and powerful. This was no rat.

Then he heard the breathing. Slow and steady, calculated and unhurried, a predator's breathing. It had hunted before, yes, and killed too. The thought made his legs weak and rubbery. He turned a corner and found himself at yet another junction, from which more passageways spread like the spokes of a wheel.

"This could go on forever."

Perhaps the beast shared his feeling that the pursuit had gone on long enough, because it chose that moment to make its move. There was a scraping sound in the gloom, the loudest yet.

He spun round. Framed in the half-light of one opening, the beast was pawing the ground.

"I'm not scared."

It wasn't true. What's more, the beast knew. His quavering voice settled on the air, painting a picture of his mounting fear. He was clutching the sword's hilt the way a drowning man clings to a piece of driftwood. For comfort. For survival. And, for the first time, he felt its weight. It made his arm shake. His strength was draining away. He tried to grip the hilt with both hands, steadying his weapon.

"Come on then, what are you waiting for?"

But still the beast stood in the archway, pawing at the floor. It was bigger than a man. It stood almost three metres tall and was massively built with slabs of muscle on its chest and shoulders. Below the waist it was bull-like. It had a swinging tail and mud splattered hooves. Or was it mud? Above the waist it was a man except, that is, for the head. And what a head! The muzzle was huge and when it opened it revealed the sharp, curved teeth, not of a bull but of a big cat. They were the fangs of a lion or tiger, made for ripping flesh. Its eyes were yellow and blazed unflinchingly through the murk. Then there were the great horns, glinting and sharp, curving from its monstrous brow. Thick and muscular as the neck was, it seemed barely able to support such a fearsome head, and strained visibly under the impossible weight.

"Oh my –"

The beast stepped out of the tunnel, and the boy actually took a few steps back. It was as if his soul had crept out of his body and was tugging at him, begging him to get away. In the sparse light shed from the gratings in the ceiling, the beast looked even more hideous. There was the sweat for a start, standing out in gleaming beads on that enormous neck and shoulders.

But that wasn't all. The creature was smeared from head to foot with filth and dried blood. It was every inch a killer. The beast began to stamp forward, its hooves clashing on the stone floor. It raised its head, the horns scraping on the ceiling, and gave a bellow that seemed to crush the air.

"I can't do this…"

He fell back, scrambling over obstacles on the floor, and fled. That's when he realised he'd dropped the ball of string. His lifeline was gone.

"Oh no!"

The beast was charging head down.
Got to get out of here!

In his mind's eye, he could see himself impaled on the points of those evil-looking horns, his legs pedalling feebly in the air, his head snapped back, his eyes growing pale and lifeless.

Suddenly he was running for his life, skidding on the slimy floor.

"Help me!"

He saw the startled brown eyes of the girl above the grating.

"Don't run!" she cried. "Fight. You must fight."

He was almost dying of shame. This wasn't supposed to happen. He wasn't meant to lose and there weren't supposed to be witnesses to his defeat.

"Fight," she repeated. "It's the way of things."

The way of things. That's right, he was meant to stand and fight. It was in his nature as a hero. But he couldn't. Not against *that*.

Alan Gibbons

What Katy Did (2)

All the morning through things seemed to go wrong. Katy missed twice in her grammar lesson, and lost her place in the class. Her hand shook so when she copied her composition, that the writing, not good at best, turned out almost illegible, so that Mrs Knight said it must be all done over again. This made Katy crosser than ever; and, almost before she thought, she had whispered to Clover, "How hateful!" And then, when just before recess all who had been speaking were requested to stand up, her conscience gave such a twinge that she was forced to get up with the rest and see a black mark put against her name on the list. The tears came into her eyes from vexation; and, for fear that the other girls would notice them, she made a bolt for the yard as soon as the bell rang, and mounted up all alone to the wood-house roof, where she sat with her back to the school, fighting with her eyes, and trying to get her face in order before the rest should come.

Miss Miller's clock was about four minutes slower than Mrs Knight's, so the next playground was empty. It was a warm, breezy day, and as Katy sat there, suddenly a gust of wind came, and seizing her sun-bonnet, which was only half tied on, whirled it across the roof. She clutched after it as it flew, but too late. Once, twice, thrice it flapped, then it disappeared over the edge, and Katy, flying after, saw it lying a crumpled lilac heap in the very middle of the enemy's yard.

This was horrible! Not merely losing the bonnet, for Katy was comfortably indifferent as to what became of her clothes, but to lose it *so*. In another minute the Miller girls would be out. Already she seemed to see them dancing war-dances round the unfortunate bonnet, pinning it on a pole, using it as a football, waving it over the fence, and otherwise treating it as Indians treat a captive taken in war. Was it to be endured? Never! Better die first! And with very much the feeling of a person who faces destruction rather than forfeit honour, Katy set her teeth, and sliding rapidly down the roof, seized the fence, and with one bold leap vaulted into Miss Miller's back yard.

Just then the recess bell tinkled; and a little Millerite who sat by the window, and who for two seconds had been dying to give the exciting information, squeaked out to the others:
"There's Katy Carr in our backyard!"

Out poured the Millerites, big and little. Their wrath and indignation at this daring invasion cannot be described. With a howl of fury they precipitated themselves upon Katy, but she was as quick as they, and holding the rescued bonnet in her hand, was already half-way up the fence. There are moments when it is a fine thing to be tall. On this occasion Katy's long arms and legs served her an excellent turn. Nothing but a Daddy Longlegs ever climbed so fast or so wildly as she did now. In one second she had gained the top of the fence. Just as she went over a Millerite seized her by the last foot, and almost dragged her boot off.

Almost, but not quite, thanks to the stout thread with which Aunt Izzie had sewed on the buttons. With a frantic kick Katy released herself, and had the satisfaction of seeing her assailant go head over heels backwards, while with a shriek of triumph and fright, she plunged herself headlong into the midst of a group of Knights.

Susan Coolidge

Five Children and It (2)

"Just one more, please," said the children. "Can you give wishes now?"

"Of course," said it; "didn't I give you yours a few minutes ago? You said, 'I wish you'd come out,' and I did."

"Oh, please, mayn't we have another?"

"Yes, but be quick about it. I'm tired of you."

I daresay you have often thought what you would do if you had three wishes given you, and have despised the old man and his wife in the black-pudding story, and felt certain that if you had the chance you could think of three really useful wishes without a moment's hesitation. These children had often talked this matter over, but, now the chance had suddenly some to them, they could not make up their minds.

"Quick," said the Sand-fairy crossly. No one could think of anything, only Anthea did manage to remember a private wish of her own and Jane's which they had never told the boys. She knew the boys would not care about it – but still it was better than nothing.

"I wish we were all as beautiful as the day," she said in a great hurry.

The children looked at each other, but each could see that the others were not any better-looking than usual. The Psammead pushed out its long eyes, and seemed to be holding its breath and swelling itself out till it was twice as fat and furry as before. Suddenly it let its breath go in a long sigh.

"I'm really afraid I can't manage it," it said apologetically; "I must be out of practice."

The children were horribly disappointed.

"Oh *do* try again!" they said.

"Well," said the Sand-fairy, "the fact is, I was keeping back a little strength to give the rest of you your wishes with. If you'll be contented with one a day amongst the lot of you I daresay I can screw myself up to it. Do you agree to that?"

"Yes, oh yes!" said Jane and Anthea. The boys nodded. They did not believe the Sand-fairy could do it. You can always make girls believe things much easier than you can boys.

It stretched out its eyes farther than ever, and swelled and swelled and swelled.

"I do hope it won't hurt itself," said Anthea.

"Or crack its skin," Robert said anxiously.

Everyone was very much relieved when the Sand-fairy, after getting so big that it almost filled up the hole in the sand, suddenly let out its breath and went back to its proper size.

"That's all right," it said, panting heavily. "It'll come easier tomorrow."

"Did it hurt much?" asked Anthea.

"Only my poor whisker, thank you," said he, "but you're a kind and thoughtful child. Good day."

It scratched suddenly and fiercely with its hands and feet, and disappeared into the sand. Then the children looked at each other, and each child suddenly found itself alone with three perfect strangers, all radiantly beautiful.

They stood for some moments in perfect silence. Each thought that its brothers and sisters had wandered off, and that these strange children had stolen up unnoticed while it was watching the swelling form of the Sand-fairy. Anthea spoke first –

"Excuse me," she said very politely to Jane, who now had enormous blue eyes and a cloud of russet hair, "but have you seen two little boys and a little girl anywhere about?"

"I was just going to ask you that," said Jane. And then Cyril cried:

"Why, it's *you*! I know the hole in your pinafore! You *are* Jane, aren't you? And you're the Panther; I can see your dirty handkerchief that you forgot to change after you'd cut your thumb! Crikey! The wish has come off, after all. I say, am I as handsome as you are?"

"If you're Cyril, I liked you much better as you were before," said Anthea decidedly. "You look like the picture of the young chorister, with your golden hair; you'll die young, I shouldn't wonder. And if that's Robert, he's like an Italian organ-grinder. His hair's all black."

"You two girls are like Christmas cards, then – that's all – silly Christmas cards," said Robert angrily. "And Jane's hair is simply carrots."

It was indeed that Venetian tint so much admired by artists.

"Well, it's no use finding fault with each other," said Anthea; "let's get the Lamb and lug it home to dinner. The servants will admire us most awfully, you'll see."

E Nesbit

Shadow of the Minotaur (2)

"That's it," he cried, throwing down his sword, "I've had enough. Game over!"

Ripping off the mask and gloves, Phoenix bent double gulping down air like it had been rationed. The dank half-light of the tunnels was replaced by the welcome glow from an Anglepoise lamp in his father's study. He glanced at the score bracelet on his wrist. It registered total defeat: **000000**. For a few moments everything was spinning, the claws of the game digging into the flesh of the here and now. Then his surroundings became reassuringly familiar.

He was out.

It was a game!

"Well?" his dad asked, "What do you think?"

"Mind-blowing," Phoenix panted. "It was all so real. It was like another world. I mean, I *was* Theseus. I went into the palace of the tyrant-king Minos. I could actually touch the stone columns, feel the heat of the braziers, smell the incense."

He knew he was gushing, babbling like a little kid, but he didn't care. "The king's daughter Ariadne helped me and she wasn't just an image on a screen. She was a real girl. Then I actually came face to face with the Minotaur. It was really happening. I believed it." He shivered. "Still do."

"Oh, I could tell how convincing it was," said Dad, enjoying the mixture of excitement and fear in his son's voice. "You were screaming your silly head off by the end. I bet your mother thought I was killing you in here."

Phoenix blushed then, beginning to control his breathing at last, he picked up the mask and gloves and traced the attached wires back to the computer where images of the labyrinth were still flashing away on the screen.

"It really was just a game?"

Dad pushed his seat back and gave a superior smile.

"That's all. Just a very sophisticated piece of software, hooked up to an even more sophisticated piece of hardware."

Scared as he had been, Phoenix didn't want it to be a game. He wanted it to be real. Real and vibrant as the old legends had always seemed to him. He fingered the soft texture of the amazing gloves and mask that had created the illusion. "And you get to play with all this great stuff for a living?"

"I certainly do. And there's a lot more to come. To quote my boss, Mr Glen Reede: *This is only one stage of development of the ultimate game.*"

Phoenix stared at the screen and the figure of the Minotaur. Is that what he'd been afraid of? That ridiculous cartoon-strip monster blinking on the screen.

"Maybe now you'll quit complaining about moving to Brownleigh."

That was asking a bit much. When Dad gave up his job at Compu-soft and accepted the lucrative offer from Magna-com, he'd fulfilled a lifelong dream. Only it was *his* lifelong dream. Phoenix and his mother had hated moving out of London, away from family and friends, especially when it meant resettling in a one-eyed backwater halfway between Dullsville and Nowhere. Life's the game, thought Phoenix, a boring game of patience.

"We could have stayed in London," Phoenix argued. "After all you're working from home. What's was wrong with the house we had?"

"Where do you want me to start?" Dad asked. "The noise, the pollution, the rat race, the crime."

Phoenix shook his head. The city had got Dad down, but he could keep his peace and quiet.

Brownleigh was a dump. No cinema, no sports centre, no railway station. There was nothing at all to do, and when it came to escaping the boredom, the buses to the nearest big town stopped at 10 o'clock. Phoenix was still trying to work out what people did around here. Maybe they took a chair onto the pavement so they could watch the traffic lights change!

He'd gone from a city that never sleeps to a town that never wakes up. That was why he couldn't forgive his dad. London was what Phoenix craved – something big and important – and Dad had taken him away from it. Dad hadn't just pulled out of the rat race, he'd just about pulled out of life.

"Anyway," said Dad, unplugging the mask and gloves from the phone socket in the PC, "We're here now so you'd better make the best of it."

Alan Gibbons

Moon Cake

The next day was sunshiny, as much as days ever were at Ware-on-the-Cliff; a mild sun peered doubtfully through the mist. Tom took an old box that had once held his grandfather's pipe tobacco and made his way up the hill, past the last houses, and the gardens full of cabbages, and the gorse bushes, to where the forest began. Great beech trees stood like the advance guard of an army; but, due to the west wind which blew so strongly for ten months of the year, they did not stand up straight, but leaned eastwards, so that the crest of them, on top of the hill, slanted like the plume on a Roman soldier's helmet.

Tom went a short way in, among the trees. He did not go far, because of the wolves. Ahead of him the forest was black dark, where the trunks clustered closer together and the canopy of leaves overhead kept out the daylight. Underfoot the soil was soft and brown and crumbly, from years of rotting leaves.

For ever, thought Tom, walking very quietly between trees. I suppose this forest has been here *for ever*. You couldn't put this forest back the way it was, because it always was.

And then he remembered his dream.

He remembered his dream because his tongue was still painfully sore. When Tom's dreams became too frightening, he bit his tongue, and woke himself out of them. Last night's dream had been one of that kind. It had taken place in a forest, but the forest was full of water. Sharks had been swimming among the trees, huge deadly sharks with black backs and white, smooth, terrifyingly under-hung jaws, full of brilliant razor-sharp teeth.

Tom paused, remembering the awfulness of his dream. He thought: perhaps, once, the sea was all over the top of this cliff, perhaps where I am now was deep under water. Was the moon still there, then? Up above?

He looked down at the ground. And he saw an active twist of adders, young adders, a whole family of them, newly hatched, wriggling and squirming, all tangled together, not a shoe's length ahead of his right foot.

He stood stock-still, his breath suspended, his skin icy with fright. Tom really hated snakes. And these were deadly ones, he knew. Not one bite, perhaps, but half-a-dozen – as there must be here – half-a-dozen snake bites could easily finish you off. Very cautiously, he took himself backwards, making a close study of every patch of ground where he intended to set foot. And so he suddenly began to notice the green-glass tree snails, shining here and there in the beech mast like tiny twinkling emerald beads. Some were on the beech roots, some on the trunks of the trees.

Tom saw more adders, as well. One lay curled up, very peacefully, fast asleep, in a tidy symmetrical flat coil, with its head in the middle. One was making its purposeful way among the beech crumble, minding its own business. One wary, uncertain, weaving its head to and fro; Tom moved well away from that one, and went in a different direction. It resembled somebody, he couldn't think who. He saw no wolves.

Joan Aiken

Dawlish Dobson

Edward felt sick. He got dressed in slow motion and had to be persuaded and cajoled every bit of the way. It was all right for Lisa and Marie. They had friends already. He was going to have to walk through a classroom door and be the only new boy in the class. Everyone would stare at him. Everyone would have their own friends and their own groups. Who would like him? Perhaps they would tease him about his sticky-out ears; perhaps they would joke about the way he spoke. Perhaps they would knock him around in the playground or trip him up. At his other school, he had been considered rather good at football, and he had many friends. Would they think so here? What a dumb, stupid thing it was to move, he thought miserably.

Mrs Thomas walked them all to school. It was a long walk, right through the village, on and on until the road turned steeply and climbed the hill past the church. The walk turned into a procession, as more and more children joined them. Edward felt conspicuous. No one else had their mothers or fathers along.

"Mum! Must you come any further? We'll be O.K.," he pleaded.

"Don't be ridiculous, Edward," said his mother firmly. "I've got to see you and the twins into school on your first day."

Then Lisa and Marie saw their new friends Chloë and Michelle and rushed ahead to catch up with them, and Edward was left walking alone beside his mother. He felt like a baby. He felt humiliated. He was sure people were noticing and staring at him. He dropped behind hoping no one would realise they were together. This hope was shattered by a loud shout. "Hey! Mrs Thomas! Hello, Edward!" It was Dawlish who rushed upon them like long lost friends and always with that sweet smile on his face which made Edward feel sick.

Of course Mrs Thomas gushed all over him. "Oh, Dawlish, how good to see you. Edward needs somebody he knows to go into school with. I hope you'll keep an eye on him for me."

"Course I will," cried Dawlish, grinning at Edward who was so embarrassed he wanted the ground to open and swallow him up.

They reached the school gates. Edward viewed them with his heart in his boots. Only the sight of the two solitary goal posts, standing like sculptures on the broad, open space of the playing field, lifted his spirits just a little.

Yet, the first day at school was not at all what Edward expected. It was terrible of course, but not in the way he had imagined. Yes, everyone did stare at him when he walked in through the classroom door; yes, they did poke fun at his accent and the way he spoke; yes, sure enough, someone did call him 'Big Ears', but the biggest surprise was the way in which they treated Dawlish. When the teacher said, "Edward, would you like to sit next to Dawlish as you seem to be friends already," everyone sniggered and someone held his nose.

"Stop it, now!" exclaimed the teacher angrily.

Jamila Gavin

The Journey

It was decided that she would make the journey alone. The school had been selected with that very purpose in mind. Her father's words could be heard echoing in her head: she had been cosseted too long, babied far too much; she had been transported by car until she was eleven, and the habit must be broken. The journey could not be avoided.

Her antipathy to walking was not easily explained. It was not walking itself that she was against: it was that stretch of walking. The journey to Stanford High did not offer many options; and each route involved crossing Clopton Bridge. It was Clopton Bridge that had to be feared.

Clopton Bridge was where the gangs congregated. It was where the way could be barred. It was where bags might be snatched and thrown about, or taunts shouted. It was where people were laughed at. It was where she dreaded. Nevertheless, how could this be explained to her father? The fears seemed babyish. It had to be faced alone.

Her holiday was wasted. It passed in a blur of anxieties: anxiety about the new work she would be set; anxiety about the new friends that would not be made; anxiety about being disliked; but most of all, anxiety about the journey. The new uniform was bought; the equipment was checked; the items on the school's list were ticked off; and the days passed.

It was at the end of August that the house next door finally became occupied. It had been empty for months, before being taken by the new family. The mother and son were invited in for a cup of tea, and she was forced to sit with them. The boy must be entertained.

The boy turned out to be her age, with a place already accepted at Stanford High. He was not like her: he was confident and assured. She knew he would become bored with her company, but he did not. He was friendly. He made a point of calling in; inviting her to his house; walking to the shop with her; and talking of his excitement at starting a new school.

Should he be told? Should his excitement be ruined? She wondered, and finally felt that he was owed the information. His reaction was unexpected: her information was greeted with laugher and dismissal. Gangs he had passed every day; taunts he was used to; threats usually evaporated. His excitement was unshaken.

She was invited to make the journey with him. It made sense: the same journey had to be made by both of them. She could learn from him and his confidence could be shared. He convinced her that the journey would become nothing, a routine part of her day. It was part of life. Once faced up to, it would be seen to be manageable.

And it did.

From **Annus Mirabilis**

The Fire of London

Such was the rise of this prodigious fire,
    Which in mean buildings first obscurely bred,
From thence did soon to open streets aspire,
    And straight to palaces and temples spread.

In this deep quiet, from what source unknown,
    Those seeds of fire their fatal birth disclose:
And first, few scattering sparks about were blown,
    Big with the flames that to our ruin rose.

Then, in some close-pent room it crept along,
    And, smouldering as it went, in silence fed:
Till th' infant monster, with devouring strong,
    Walked boldly upright with exalted head.

At length the crackling noise and dreadful blaze,
    Called up some waking lover to the sight;
And long it was ere he the rest could raise,
    Whose heavy eye-lids yet were full of night.

The next to danger, hot pursu'd by fate,
    Half clothed, half naked, hastily retire:
And frighted mothers strike their breasts, too late,
    For helpless infants left amidst the fire.

Their cries soon waken all the dwellers near:
    Now murmuring noises rise in every street:
The more remote run stumbling with their fear,
    And, in the dark, men justle as they meet.

Now streets grow thronged and busy as by day:
    Some run for buckets to the hallowed choir:
Some cut the pipes, and some the engines play,
    And some more bold mount ladders to the fire.

In vain: for, from the East, a *Belgian* wind,
    His hostile breath through the dry rafters sent:
The flames impelled, soon left their foes behind,
    And forward, with a wanton fury went.

A key of fire ran all along the shore,
    And lightened all the river with the blaze:
The wakened tides began again to roar,
    And wondering fish in shining waters gaze.

The fire, meantime, walks in a broader gross,
    To either hand his wings he opens wide:
He wades the streets, and straight he reaches cross,
    And plays his longing flames on th'other side.

At first they warm, then scorch, and then they take:
    Now with long necks from side to side they feed:
At length, grown strong, their mother fire forsake,
    And a new colony of flames succeed.

To every nobler portion of the town,
    The curling billows roll their restless tide:
In parties now they straggle up and down,
    As armies, unopposed, for prey divide.

John Dryden

Again

Slowly starting:
Days shortening,
Sunlight shifting,
Flowers shrinking;
Trees shedding.
Scale dropping,
Animals hiding,
Birds fleeing.
People feeling
Winter gripping.

Lengthening light
Pushing perennials,
Stirring sleepers,
Welcoming deserters;
Colouring trees,
Painting flowers,
Strengthening rays;
Lifting spirits,
Freeing children
Relishing summer.

The Road Not Taken

Two roads diverged in a yellow wood,
And sorry I could not travel both
And be one traveller, long I stood
And looked down one as far as I could
To where it bent in the undergrowth;

Then took the other, as just as fair,
And having perhaps the better claim,
Because it was grassy and wanted wear;
Though as for that the passing there
Had worn them really about the same,

And both that morning equally lay
In leaves no step had trodden black.
Oh, I kept the first for another day!
Yet knowing how way leads on to way,
I doubted if I should ever come back.

I shall be telling this with a sigh
Somewhere ages and ages hence;
Two roads diverged in a wood, and I –
I took the one less travelled by,
And that has made all the difference.

Robert Frost

The Donkey

When fishes flew and forests walked
    And figs grew upon thorn,
Some moment when the moon was blood
    Then surely I was born.

With monstrous head and sickening cry
    And ears like errant wings,
The devil's walking parody
    On all four-footed things.

The tattered outlaw of the earth,
    Of ancient crooked will;
Starve, scourge, deride me: I am dumb,
    I keep my secret still.

Fools! For I also had my hour;
    One far fierce hour and sweet;
There was a shout about my ears,
    And palms before my feet.

G K Chesterton

POETRY | ROBERT LOUIS STEVENSON

Text 38

Escape at Bedtime

The lights from the parlour and kitchen shone out
   Through the blinds and the windows and bars;
And high overhead and all moving about,
   There were thousands of millions of stars.
There ne'er were such thousands of leaves on a tree,
   Nor of people in church or the Park,
As the crowds of the stars that looked down upon me,
   And that glittered and winked in the dark.

The Dog, and the Plough, and the Hunter, and all,
   And the star of the sailor, and Mars,
These shone in the sky, and the pail by the wall
   Would be half full of water and stars.
They saw me at last, and they chased me with cries,
   And they soon had me packed into bed;
But the glory kept shining and bright in my eyes,
   And the stars going round in my head.

Robert Louis Stevenson

POETRY | ROBERT LOUIS STEVENSON

Text 39

The Moon

The moon has a face like the clock in the hall;
She shines on thieves on the garden wall,
On streets and fields and harbour quays,
And birdies asleep in the forks of the trees.

The squalling cat and the squeaking mouse,
The howling dog by the door of the house,
The bat that lies in bed at noon,
All love to be out by the light of the moon.

But all of the things that belong to the day
Cuddle to sleep to be out of her way;
And flowers and children close their eyes
Till up in the morning the sun shall arise.

Robert Louis Stevenson

The Moon

The moon was but a chin of gold
  A night or two ago,
And now she turns her perfect face
  Upon the world below.

Her forehead is of amplest blond;
  Her cheek like beryl stone;
Her eye unto the summer dew
  The likest I have known.

Her lips of amber never part;
  But what must be the smile
Upon her friend she could bestow
  Were such her silver will!

And what a privilege to be
  But the remotest star!
For certainly her way might pass
  Beside your twinkling door.

Her bonnet is a firmament,
  The universe her shoe,
The stars the trinkets at her belt,
  Her dimities of blue.

Emily Dickinson

POETRY | EMILY DICKINSON

Evening

She sweeps with many-coloured brooms,
And leaves the shreds behind;
Oh, housewife in the evening west,
Come back, and dust the pond.

You dropped a purple ravelling in,
You dropped an amber thread;
And now you've littered all the East
With duds of emerald!

And still she plies her spotted brooms,
And still the aprons fly,
Till brooms fade softly into stars –
And then I come away.

Emily Dickinson

Black Beauty

"Are you never going to get those horses' heads up, York? Raise them at once, and let us have no more of this humouring and nonsense."

York came to me first, whilst the groom stood at Ginger's head. He drew my head back and fixed the rein so tight that it was almost intolerable; then he went to Ginger, who was impatiently jerking her head up and down against the bit, as was her way now. She had a good idea of what was coming, and the moment York took the rein off the terret in order to shorten it, she took her opportunity, and reared up so suddenly that York had his nose roughly hit, and his hat knocked off; the groom was nearly thrown off his legs. At once they both flew to her head, but she was a match for them, and went on plunging, rearing, and kicking in a most desperate manner; at last she kicked right over the carriage pole and fell down, after giving me a severe blow on my near quarter. There is no knowing what further mischief she might have done, had not York promptly sat himself down flat on her head to prevent her struggling, at the same time calling out, "Unbuckle the black horse! run for the winch and unscrew the carriage pole; cut the trace here, somebody, if you can't unhitch it." One of the footmen ran for the winch, and another brought a knife from the house. The groom soon set me free from Ginger and the carriage, and led me to my box. He just turned me in as I was and ran back to York. I was much excited by what had happened, and if I had ever been used to kick or rear, I am sure I should have done it then; but I never had, and there I stood angry, sore in my leg, my head still strained up to the terret on the saddle, and no power to get it down. I was very miserable, and felt much inclined to kick the first person who came near me.

Before long, however, Ginger was led in by two grooms, a good deal knocked about and bruised. York came with her and gave his orders, and then came to look at me. In a moment he let down my head.

"Confound these bearing reins!" he said to himself; "I thought we should have some mischief soon – master will be sorely vexed; but there – if a woman's husband can't rule her, of course a servant can't; so I wash my hands of it, and if she can't get to the Duchess' garden party, I can't help it."

York did not say this before the men; he always spoke respectfully when they were by. Now, he felt me all over, and soon found the place above my hock where I had been kicked. It was swelled and painful; he ordered it to be sponged with hot water, and then some lotion was put on.

Lord W– was much put out when he learned what had happened; he blamed York for giving way to his mistress, to which he replied that in future he would much prefer to receive his orders only from his lordship; but I think nothing came of it, for things went on the same as before. I thought York might have stood up better for his horses, but perhaps I am no judge.

Ginger was never put into the carriage again but when she was well of her bruises, one of Lord W– 's younger sons said he should like to have her; he was sure she would make a good hunter. As for me, I was obliged still to go in the carriage, and had a fresh partner called Max; he had always been used to the tight rein. I asked him how it was he bore it.

"Well," he said, "I bear it because I must, but it is shortening my life, and it will shorten yours too, if you have to stick to it."

Anna Sewell

Why the Whales Came (2)

We did all we could to discourage the whales from coming in too close to the shore. Shouting and screaming at the water's edge, we hurled stones and driftwood at them but most fell far short and those few that did hit them did not seem to deter them. The Birdman's flock of gulls wheeled noisily overhead, but the whales took no notice of them either. All the time they were drifting closer and closer to the beach and disaster. Every faint whistle from the stranded whale seemed to drive the others out in the bay to distraction, sending them rolling and plunging in amongst each other and precipitating a chorus of thunderous snorting and whistling that subsided only when the whale lay still and silent again on the sand. But each furious flurry of activity left them that much nearer the shore and there seemed nothing we could do now to stop them beaching themselves.

"Gracie," said the Birdman, "you go back to the whale and try to keep her happy. Stroke her, Gracie. Talk to her, sing to her, anything so's she doesn't call out." And he took off his sou'wester and handed it to me. "It won't do to let her get too dry either, Gracie. You can use this for a bucket."

So I went back and forth from the water's edge to the whale with the Birdman's sou'wester full of water. I began at her head, pouring the water all over her eyes and mouth. She seemed to relish it, blinking and rolling her head from side to side as the water ran down over her skin and into the sand, and all the while I talked to her quietly. I remember thinking as I looked into her eyes that she could understand me, that she could understand every word I said.

I was kneeling in the sand beside her head, stroking her behind the blowhole above her eyes, when I saw them coming back. They were hurrying along the path under Gweal Hill, Big Tim running out in front. It looked as if he had brought most of the island with him. Everyone had a weapon of some kind in his hand, a fork, an axe, a hoe or scythe; and Daniel's father carried a harpoon over his shoulder. I looked for Mother amongst them but could not pick her out. The Vicar was there, his cassock tucked up into his trousers and Mr Wellbeloved was there too, striding out with his stick alongside Daniel's father.

"Stay where you are, Gracie," the Birdman told me, "and keep her quiet if you can." By the time they reached the beach, the Birdman, Daniel and Prince stood between them and the stranded whale. No one spoke for a moment. They all stood looking incredulously at the Birdman and the whale, at Daniel and me, whispering anxiously amongst themselves. It was only when they noticed the rolling black backs breaking the water out in the bay that they began to talk aloud.

"See," Big Tim shouted in triumph, point his machete. "Didn't I tell you? Didn't I tell you? There's dozens of them out there. I said there was."

"It's a narwhal," said Mr Wellbeloved. "Yes, I do believe it's a narwhal. Well I never. Only the males have tusks, you know. He's a long way from home. That's the kind of whale that the Eskimos hunt off Greenland. Quite what he's doing here I cannot imagine. If I might take a closer look…" As he stepped towards us Prince began to growl, his lip curling back about his teeth, his neck tense with fury. Mr Wellbeloved stopped where he stood.

"Look here, Mr Woodcock," Daniel's father said, taking Mr Wellbeloved's arm and pulling him back, "we don't much care what this thing is. Whale, narwhal, it doesn't matter to us. All that matters is that there's meat on it and ivory too by the look of it. That's money to us, Mr Woodcock. Anything washed up on our beaches is ours by right, always has been, Mr Woodcock; you know that." The Birdman said nothing but looked along the ranks of islanders that faced him.

Michael Morpurgo

The Mouse and his Child

"Where are we?" the mouse child asked his father. His voice was tiny in the stillness of the night.

"I don't know," the father answered.

"*What* are we, Papa?"

"I don't know. We must wait and see."

"What astonishing ignorance!" said the clockwork elephant. "But of course you're new. I've been here such a long time that I'd forgotten how it was. Now, then," she said, "this place is a toyshop, and you are toy mice. People are going to come and buy you for children, because it's almost a time called Christmas."

"Why haven't they bought you?" asked the little tin seal. "How come you've stayed here so long?"

"It isn't quite the same for me, my dear," replied the elephant. "I'm part of the establishment, you see, and this is my house."

The house was certainly grand enough for her, or indeed for anyone. The very cornices and carven brackets bespoke a residence of dignity and style, and the dolls never set foot outside it. They had no need to; everything they could possibly want was there, from the covered platters and silver chafing dishes on the sideboard to the ebony grand piano among the potted ferns in the conservatory. No expense had been spared, and no detail was wanting. The house had rooms for every purpose, all opulently furnished and appropriately occupied: there were a piano-teacher doll and a young-lady-pupil doll in the conservatory, a nursemaid doll for the children dolls in the nursery, and a cook and butler doll in the kitchen. Interminable-weekend-guest dolls lay in all the guest room beds, sporting dolls played billiards in the billiard room, and a scholar doll in the library never ceased perusal of the book he held, although he kept in touch with the world by the hand he lightly rested on the globe that stood beside him. There was even an astronomer doll in the lookout observatory, who tirelessly aimed his little telescope at one of the automatic fire sprinklers in the ceiling of the shop. In the dining room, beneath a glittering chandelier, a party of lady and gentleman dolls sat perpetually around a table. Whatever the cook and butler might hope to serve them, they had never taken anything but tea, and that from empty cups, while plaster cakes and pastry, defying time, stood by the silver teapot on the white damask cloth.

It was the elephant's constant delight to watch that tea party through the window, and as the hostess she took great pride in the quality of her hospitality. "Have another cup of tea," she said to one of the ladies. "Try a little pastry."

"HIGH-SOCIETY SCANDAL, changing to cloudy, with a possibility of BARGAINS GALORE!" replied the lady. Her papier-mâché head being made of paste and newsprint, she always spoke in scraps of news and advertising, in whatever order they came to mind.

"Bucket seats," remarked the gentleman next to her. "Power steering optional. GOVERNMENT FALLS."

The mouse child was still thinking of what the elephant had said before. "What happens when they buy you?" he asked her.

"That, of course, is outside my experience," said the elephant, "but I should think that one simply goes out into the world and does whatever one does. One dances or balances a ball, as the case may be."

The child remembered the bitter wind that had blown in through the door, and the great staring face of the tramp at the window with the grey winter sky behind him. Now that sky was a silent darkness beyond the street lamp and the white flakes falling. The dolls' house was bright and warm; the teapot gleamed upon the dazzling cloth. "I don't want to go out into the world," he said.

"Obviously the child isn't properly brought up," said the elephant to the gentleman doll nearest her. "But then how could he be, poor thing, without a mother's guidance?"

"PRICES SLASHED," said the gentleman. "EVERYTHING MUST GO."

"You're quite right," said the elephant. "Everything must, in one way or another, go. One does what one is wound to do. It is expected of me that I walk up and down in front of my house; it is expected of you that you drink tea. And it is expected of this young mouse that he go out into the world with his father and dance in a circle."

"But I don't want to," said the mouse child, and he began to cry. It was an odd, little, tinny, rasping, sound, and father and son both rattled with it.

Russell Hoban

Magnus Powermouse

Madeleine was a country girl. You could hear it in her speech, especially when she was excited. She carefully examined the new arrivals and then suddenly drew back, her black eyes round with surprise, her hair on end.

"Crumbs!" cried Madeleine loudly. "Just look at thik girt hummock!" And had there been others there to look, they would have seen five normal newborn pink babies, each the size of a little finger-nail, and a sixth that was newborn and pink but most definitely not normal, so huge and strong and active was it.

Already, at half an hour of age, it was beginning to crawl blindly about the nest, steam-rolling its way over its brothers and sisters, and lifting its blunt snout hungrily in the air.

"Crumbs!" said Madeleine again. "He's as big as a baby rat! Whatever will his father say?"

The father of the six was a mouse of a different colour. Not only had he a dark grey coat, in contrast to Madeleine's warm brown, but he had come originally from a very different background. He had been born in fact behind the panelling of a room in an Oxford college, and had travelled down to Somerset as a youngster, quite by mistake, in a trunk full of clothes. The occupant of the room had been a Professor of Classics, and with such a history of culture behind him Madeleine's husband considered himself several cuts above country mice. His name was Marcus Aurelius.

Marcus Aurelius had his own private den, close to the sitting room fireplace. Later that day he rose from his bed of torn newspaper, where he had been reading snippets of the *Western Daily Press*. He made his way down the passage behind the sitting room wainscot that led to the family home. This was in a hole in the wall at the back of the larder. It was the beginning of winter, and as usual they had come into the warmth of the cottage from their summer residence under the raised wooden floor of the pigsty at the bottom of the garden.

He found his wife, looking, it seemed to him, rather worried, sitting in the middle of her nest. Of babies he could see no sign.

"Well, Maddie my dear," he said, peering short-sightedly, for reading in a bad light had weakened his eyes, "when are we to hear the patter of tiny feet?"

"Oh Markie, Markie!" cried Madeleine in a distracted voice. "Tidden the patter of tiny feet we shall hear. Tis the thunder of hugeous girt big 'uns!" And she rolled upon her side to show what lay beneath her.

Marcus Aurelius gave a squeak of amazement at the sight which met his myopic eyes. Five feeble babies, already more blue than pink, fumbled weakly in search of their mother's milk; but in vain. Only too plainly it had all been drunk, by the red swollen sausage-shaped monster that lay distended in the centre of the nest. And even as the horrified father watched, the giant baby bestirred itself, bullocking its way through the others and knocking them flying as it made once more for the milk-bar.

At last Marcus Aurelius found his voice, after a fashion. Normally long-winded, the shock reduced him to a series of gasps.

"Never in all my... what on earth... how?" he gulped.

"Oh, Markie," said Madeleine in low tones, as though fearful that the huge infant might overhear her. "I've never seen such a big 'un neither. And it ain't a changeling, if that's what you're thinking, it's mine all right, I should know. And as for 'how', I can't rightly tell. Must be something I ate."

Dick King-Smith

The Amazing Maurice and his Educated Rodents

They said he was amazing. The Amazing Maurice, they said. He'd never meant to be amazing. It had just happened.

He'd realized something was odd that day, just after lunch, when he'd looked into a reflection in a puddle and thought *that's me*. He'd never been *aware* of himself before. Of course, it was hard to remember *how* he'd thought before he became amazing. It seemed to him that his mind had been just a kind of soup.

And then there had been the rats, who lived under the rubbish heap in one corner of his territory. He'd realised there was something educated about the rats when he jumped on one and it'd said, "Can we talk about this?", and part of his amazing new brain had told him you couldn't eat someone who could talk. At least, not until you'd heard what they'd got to say.

The rat had been Peaches. She wasn't like other rats. Nor were Dangerous Beans, Donut Enter, Darktan, Hamnpork, Big Savings, Toxie and all the rest of them. But, then, Maurice wasn't like other cats any more.

Other cats were, suddenly, *stupid*. Maurice started to hang around with the rats, instead. They were someone to talk to. He got on fine so long as he remembered not to eat anyone they knew.

The rats spent a lot of time worrying about why *they* were suddenly so clever. Maurice considered that this was a waste of time. Stuff happened. But the rats went on and on about whether it was something on the rubbish heap that they'd eaten, and even Maurice could see that wouldn't explain how *he'd* got changed, because he'd never eaten rubbish. And he certainly wouldn't eat any rubbish off *that* heap, seeing as where it came from…

He considered that the rats were, quite frankly, dumb. Clever, OK, but *dumb*. Maurice had lived on the streets for four years and barely had any ears left and scars all over his nose, and he was *smart*. He swaggered so much when he walked that if he didn't slow down he flipped himself over. When he fluffed out his tail people had to step around it. He reckoned you had to be smart to live for four years on these streets, especially with all the dog gangs and freelance furriers. One wrong move and you were lunch and a pair of gloves. Yes, you *had* to be smart.

You also had to be rich. This took some explaining to the rats, but Maurice had roamed the city and learned how things worked and money, he said, was the key to everything.

And then one day he'd seen the stupid-looking kid playing the flute with his cap in front of him for pennies, and he'd had an idea. An amazing idea. It just turned up, bang, all at once. Rats, flute, stupid-looking kid…

And he'd said, "Hey, stupid-looking kid! How would you like to make your fortu– nah, kid, I'm down here…"

Terry and Lyn Pratchett

The War of Jenkins' Ear

The rice-pudding was as good as it looked – it always was. Toby searched for a morsel of skin in his helping, his favourite bit, but found none.

"You like skin?" said a voice from across the table. It was the new boy, Christopher. How he knew that Toby liked the skin Toby could not make out. "You can have mine then," said Christopher. "I can't stand skin." He stood up, leaned across the table and scooped the skin on to Toby's plate – not at all the sort of thing you were supposed to do at Redlands. Toby looked down the table. It was all right. Mr Birley hadn't noticed. Toby was savouring his first mouthful of rice-pudding skin when the gong sounded behind him from the High Table. The dining-hall fell silent at once. Rudolph rose to his feet slowly, pushing himself up on his knuckles.

"That new boy on the window table," he said, his eyes narrowing. "Christopher, isn't it? Stand up will you. On the bench. And Jenkins, you too."

Toby knew at once what it would be about, but he could see that Christopher was completely bewildered. Toby could feel his heart pounding in his ears as he stepped on to the bench and faced Mr Stagg. He'd only been back at school an hour or two and he was already in the middle of a nightmare.

"I don't know," Rudolph began, his voice full of acid menace. "I don't know what sort of a home you have come from, what sort of a school you have come from; but here at Redlands we do not lean across the table, we eat what is put in front of us and we do not turn our noses up at Mrs Woolland's excellent rice-pudding. 'Manners maketh man' is the motto of one of our great schools, and at Redlands we set great store by our manners, Christopher. Now, as this is your first meal with us I am prepared to turn a blind eye, but just this once. If ever I see you…"

"I don't eat the skin, sir." Christopher spoke quietly. It was very matter of fact. There was no defiance in his tone.

"I beg your pardon," said Rudolph, his brow twitching with irritation.

"I like the rest of it, sir," Christopher explained coolly, "but I don't eat the skin. I never do."

"Do you not?" Rudolph said smiling thinly. "Well, I'm afraid, Christopher, we will have to teach you an early lesson and it is this. Here you will do what you are told to do, not what you feel like doing. Food at Redlands is always eaten whether you like it or not and without complaint. We do not waste our food at Redlands, do you hear me?"

"Yes, sir, I know, sir. It was the same at my last school. That's why I gave it to him, sir, so it wouldn't be wasted."

No one in the dining hall could believe what they were witnessing. It was quite unthinkable for a boy to argue the toss with Rudolph. With Rudolph there was safety only in silent, abject acceptance. Rudolph roused was a very dangerous animal and every boy in the school knew it.

Michael Morpurgo

Harry Potter and the Order of the Phoenix

The Hat became motionless once more; applause broke out, though it was punctured, for the first time in Harry's memory, with muttering and whispers. All across the Great Hall students were exchanging remarks with their neighbours, and Harry, clapping along with everyone else, knew exactly what they were talking about.

"Branched out a bit this year, hasn't it?" said Ron, his eyebrows raised.

"Too right it has," said Harry.

The Sorting Hat usually confined itself to describing the different qualities looked for by each of the four Hogwarts houses and its own role in Sorting them. Harry could not remember it ever trying to give the school advice before.

"I wonder if it's ever given warnings before?" said Hermione, sounding slightly anxious.

"Yes, indeed," said Nearly Headless Nick knowledgeably, leaning across Neville towards her (Neville winced; it was very uncomfortable to have a ghost lean through you). "The Hat feels itself honour-bound to give the school due warning whenever it feels – "

But Professor McGonagall, who was waiting to read out the list of first-years' names, was giving the whispering students the sort of look that scorches. Nearly Headless Nick placed a see-through finger to his lips and sat primly upright again as the muttering came to an abrupt end. With a last frowning look that swept the four house tables, Professor McGonagall lowered her eyes to her long piece of parchment and called out the first name.

"Abercrombie, Euan."

The terrified-looking boy Harry had noticed earlier stumbled forwards and put the Hat on his head; it was only prevented from falling right down to his shoulders by his very prominent ears. The Hat considered for a moment, then the rip near the brim opened again and shouted:

"Gryffindor!"

Harry clapped loudly with the rest of Gryffindor house as Euan Abercrombie staggered to their table and sat down, looking as though he would like very much to sink through the floor and never be looked at again.

Slowly, the long line of first-years thinned. In the pauses between the names and the Sorting Hat's decisions, Harry could hear Ron's stomach rumbling loudly. Finally, "Zeller, Rose" was Sorted into Hufflepuff, and Professor McGonagall picked up the Hat and stool and marched them away as Professor Dumbledore rose to his feet.

Whatever his recent bitter feelings had been towards his Headmaster, Harry was somehow soothed to see Dumbledore standing before them all. Between the absence of Hagrid and the presence of those dragonish horses, he had felt that his return to Hogwarts, so long anticipated, was full of unexpected surprises, like jarring notes in a familiar song. But this, at least, was how it was supposed to be: their Headmaster rising to greet them all before the start-of-term feast.

"To our newcomers," said Dumbledore in a ringing voice, his arms stretched wide and a beaming smile on his lips, "welcome! To our old hands – welcome back! There is a time for speech-making, but this is not it. Tuck in!"

There was an appreciative laugh and an outbreak of applause as Dumbledore sat down neatly and threw his long beard over his shoulder so as to keep it out of the way of his plate – for food had appeared out of nowhere, so that the five long tables were groaning under joints and pies and dishes of vegetables, bread and sauces and flagons of pumpkin juice.

"Excellent," said Ron, with a kind of groan of longing, and he seized the nearest plate of chops and began piling them on to his plate, watched wistfully by Nearly Headless Nick.

"What were you saying before the Sorting?" Hermione asked the ghost. "About the Hat giving warnings?"

"Oh, yes," said Nick, who seemed glad of a reason to turn away from Ron, who was now eating roast potatoes with almost indecent enthusiasm. "Yes, I have heard the Hat give several warnings before, always at times when it detects periods of great danger for the school. And always, of course, its advice is the same: stand together, be strong from within."

J K Rowling

EXTENDED NARRATIVE

Text 49

Changing Places

She had known it would be like this. She had warned Mum. In spite of that, Mum had insisted on moving, saying it would give them a new start in life; then they could both forget everything that had happened. However, it was not as easy as that. They had come to the most boring, miserable place, and they had brought their memories with them. What is more, she was now at school. The school was far bigger than Brookhurst. It had 400 children, and Emma felt as if they were all staring at or talking about her. She knew no one. She had spent two weeks helping Mum to unpack, before being plunged into this. Now she had to get through the day.

A whistle suddenly shrieked. Breaking off from her miserable thoughts, Emma looked about her. Everyone had started moving, heading towards one of two doors. This was the first test: which was the right door? Emma followed behind children who looked about her age. Suddenly, a sharp jolt in the back sent her sprawling, her bag flying in one direction, her lunch-box in the other. As she got up, she heard sniggers from a group of girls in front of her.

She made her way even more miserably towards the door, where a teacher was waiting. A whistle dangled from his hand, as he drank a cup of coffee.

"I'm new," she said quietly. "I'm supposed to go to Mrs Doyle's class."

"And I'm thirsty," replied the teacher, "so don't bother me now. Tracey, take this girl with you lot."

Emma's heart sank: Tracey was one of the sniggering group. However, Tracey's reply was surprisingly cheerful.

"We'll look after her, Mr Harbin," she simpered, but, as Tracey turned away from the teacher, Emma recognised a look that was far from friendly.

The walk to the classroom was perhaps ten metres, so it did not give the opportunity for a long conversation. Nevertheless, it gave ample time for these girls: they used it as an opportunity to set Emma straight.

"So, you're in our class, are you? Well, you'd better learn who we are pretty quickly. I'm Tracey; she's Cassie; that's Laura; and…"

"I'm Beth," interrupted the tallest of the group. "What's more, I'm the leader of this class, and this is my gang. We don't take any messing about, and we don't like people getting in our way."

With that, Beth elbowed Emma to one side, and made her way into a classroom. As she entered, the noise subsided. Beth was the undisputed leader, and even the adult in the room seemed intimidated.

Mrs Doyle proved far less awe-inspiring than 'Beth's Gang'. The teacher was friendly and helpful. After showing Emma where to hang her jacket, she allocated her a place in the classroom. Never had Emma been so relieved to find herself sitting at the front of a classroom. Normally, she liked grabbing a place at the back, where it was easy to have a chat or a quick daydream when lessons became boring; in this classroom, as long as she was kept away from Beth and her cronies, it was a blessing. Perhaps fortunately, she did not know yet what playtime had in store for her…

Goodnight Mr Tom

Mr Bush dealt with the older children first and placed a few evacuees with them at the back. It was very noisy. There was a lot of shouting and shuffling amongst the newcomers, most of whom were feeling bored and restless and had spent too long in the country already.

Mr Bush announced the times when the older ones were next needed and dismissed them.

George, Carrie and Ginnie were to be in Mrs Hartridge's class again. She was taking the eight- to eleven-year-olds. The twins had had their tenth birthday in the holidays and George was eleven.

Mrs Black was to have all the local children and non-Catholic evacuees from five years old to eight.

Willie watched Mrs Hartridge approach him and Zach. Zach told her his age, which was nine, and spelt out his name, apologizing for it at the same time. She smiled. Willie handed her his label and said nothing. Her long flaxen hair was coiled up in a thick plait at the top of her head. Willie gazed with pleasure at her soft, pink-cheeked face and then suddenly his heart fell.

She leaned over to Zach and said, "Now, Zacharias."

"You can call me Zach if it's too much of a mouthful."

"I think I can manage, thank you. Now tell me, what were you doing at your last school? You can read and write, can't you?"

At this juncture, Willie's ears filled up. Zach's chattering was only a faint rumbling echo in the distance. He felt her hand on his shoulder.

"Now, William," she said. "How about you? Can you read and write?"

He remained silent. He didn't dare look at the others. What would they think of him?

"No," he answered, and he picked at one of the nails on his fingers and stared at the floorboards wishing he could disappear into them.

"Oh, I'm sorry about that, William. I would have liked you in my class. You'll have to go and sit with Mrs Black's class," and she pointed to the little ones seated on the floor. Willie looked up in anguish and quickly sat down again.

The burning inside his ears seemed to spread into his jaw. He rose as if in a daze, found a space on the floor and sat down. He clasped his hands tightly together and bowed his head. He felt utterly humiliated.

Mrs Hartridge's class were dismissed. They were to have school in the afternoons and wouldn't be starting until Friday.

Willie was left with Mrs Black and she and the remaining children filed over to the school. There were two girls even older than him who also couldn't read, but it didn't make him feel any better. One of them ignored everyone including Mrs Black and just filed her nails and stared out of the window.

Tom was weeding the graveyard when Willie returned. He watched his dejected figure walk past him into the cottage and, after allowing a few minutes to elapse, followed him in and discovered him sitting at the table in the living room, his bag of apples and sandwich lying untouched.

"I could just do with a cuppa," he said brightly. "You too, William?"

Willie gave a nod.

He pushed a mug of tea towards him. "How was it then?"

Willie scraped the toes of his boots together.

"Bad, was it?"

Willie nodded.

"Best tell me then."

He raised his head. It was difficult to look at Tom without his lips trembling.

"I'm with the babies."

"Oh, and whose class is Zacharias in then?"

"Mrs Hartridge's."

"Why ent you? You're near enuff the same age, ent you?"

"Yeh, but he can read." He paused. "And write."

Michelle Magorian

Teaching notes and ideas

TERM 1

Poetry

Allan Ahlberg

1 Who Knows?

Discuss meanings. (Superficial argument about whether another person knows a secret; deeper meaning about an individual's unique thoughts.) Do you find the poem effective? Why? **T3**

Stress the absence of nouns. Which type of word replaces them? (Pronouns.) Revise pronouns, and ask the children to identify them and the verbs linked to them. **S1**

2 It is a Puzzle

Hold a general discussion, rather than focusing on named children. What is the puzzle? (Working out another person's thoughts.) How do you respond to the poem? **T3**

Is there a link with Text 1? (Interest in people's thoughts.) **T4**

Give practice in identifying pronouns and other word classes. **S1**

Benjamin Zephaniah

3 For Word

Why is the poem apt for a poet? (Words are the essential tools of his trade.) Hold more than one oral reading. Which words do you find memorable? Why? **T3**

Share responses to the poem. Encourage the children to refer to the text. **T5**

4 Pencil Me In

Is there a link with the message in Text 3? (Enjoyment of words; recognition of words as a means to express everything in one's life.) Which poem do you prefer? Why? **T3, T4**

Identify literal links between the word 'pencil' in the title, and vocabulary in the poem. ('Draws a line'; 'lead'; 'point'; 'grey'.) Put forward the view that the pencil is treated almost as a person. Where is this apparent?

Explain personification (a metaphor in which the language of human actions is used about objects or ideas); help the children to identify relevant active verbs ('sees'; 'tries'; 'touches'; 'fought'). **T10**

Hold group discussions on Zephaniah's poems. Compare the two poets' work. Is there a theme connection? (Expressing one's thoughts.) How is the theme treated differently? (For Zephaniah, thoughts have written expression; for Ahlberg, they remain secret.) Could this reflect the poets' personalities? Provide other examples of their work. In discussions, encourage contributions and response to what is said. **T4, T5**

Ask the children to write their own poems on the theme of thought expression, including examples of active verbs and personification. **T10**

Speaking and listening

Hold group discussions on how poems should be performed orally. Consider appropriate revisions. Share presentations.

TEACHING NOTES AND IDEAS

Narrative writing 1

5 Why the Whales Came (1)
This is an opening chapter. How much information is given? Which questions are answered? ('Who?', 'What?', 'Where?' and 'Why?') Point out that 'when' is unclear: the reader knows only that the narrator is recounting past events.

Put the children in twos to analyse the opening two paragraphs of stories they have written. Which questions are answered? Could the openings be improved? **T7**

6 The Sheep-Pig (1)
This is taken from Chapter 5. What or who do you think is new in this extract? Are problems still being introduced? (Sheep rustlers, danger of being stolen, Babe's ability to control sheep.) Model write the author's plan, encompassing this part of the story.

Ask the children to map quickly a story plan on a chosen theme. **T7**

7 The Hundred and One Dalmatians
This is taken from further into a story. Which phrase links with the preceding text ('no longer'). Point out problems needing resolution (Missis finding her way; getting food; coping with Pongo's injury). Discuss the need for complications and predicaments. **T7**

Revise different word classes, asking the children to identify examples. **S1**

Return to the plans from Text 6. Are additions needed? Are there complications that need resolving during the course of the story? **T7**

> ### Speaking and listening
> Discuss the plot, characters and structure of your class novel. Ensure that the children are familiar with appropriate terminology.
>
> Edit examples of ambiguous, complex sentences. Discuss how to clarify meanings.

Media and plays

> Texts 5–7 from Unit 2 (Narrative writing 1) can also be used as part of Unit 3 (Media and plays) in conjunction with the teaching notes below.

5 Why the Whales Came (1)
Watch the film based on Text 5. Ask the children to evaluate the two forms.

6 The Sheep-Pig (1)
Use this for adaptation to a play script. Stress the use of precise stage directions. **T9**

7 The Hundred and One Dalmatians
Have you seen the film version? How did it compare? Are there disadvantages to a film? (Loss of narrator; faster pace; interference with personal visual images.) **T1**

This story is in the third person, the author recounting the tale. Could one of the characters effectively take the role of narrator? Brainstorm ideas, and ask the children to write new versions, in the voices of two of the characters. **T6**

8 Peter Pan and Wendy
Investigate the detailed descriptions ('in a hollow voice'; 'almost gibbering'). Ask the children to list the events covered.

Focus on punctuation. Discuss when and why semicolons are used. Use the sentences as models for further writing. **S6**

9 Peter Pan (the motion picture event)
Compare this with the previous text. Note the quick tally of dead pirates, without the previous detail. Discuss how a visual film makes description less necessary. Which text do the children prefer? Is this one satisfying, without seeing the film? **T1**

10 The Witches
Stress the use of the first person as narrator. Who is 'I'? (The boy.) Examine the detail and the way in which the reader shares the narrator's thoughts. Ask the children to rewrite the narrative, using a witch as narrator. **T6**

11 The Witches: Plays for Children
How does this differ from Text 10? (The speed at which the story moves.) Analyse omissions and additions. Stress stage directions. Are they as effective as Dahl's narrative? Do you prefer Text 10 or 11? Why?

Experiment with adapting Text 9 into a play. **T9**

> **Speaking and listening**
>
> Discuss the relative impact of text and film.
>
> Use one of the texts for role-play. Question the characters about events.

Narrative writing 2

12 The Story of Tracy Beaker
What do the children learn about Tracy? (Past experiences; behaviour; personality; feelings). Is her role as narrator relevant? Can she be drawn as effectively on screen? (A realistic evaluation should be possible from the BBC television series.) **T1, T2**

Rewrite this extract with a different narrator. Has the point of view changed? **T6**

Analyse Wilson's writing: her ability to move the plot forward, while simultaneously revealing details about the past; her unconventional, unpredictable plots; her attitude to her characters. **T7**

Focus on language, using the text for identification of different word classes. **S1**

13 My Friend Walter
What is the author doing in this narrative opening? (Introducing characters.) What is the first hint of a plot complication? (Arrival of the postcard.) **T7**

Analyse writing style. Are most sentences simple or complex? (Simple – to suit the voice of a 10-year-old girl.) Try creating complex sentences, revising different connecting devices. Which links work best? Does clause sequence affect meaning? **S5**

Brainstorm themes for the children's writing. Ask them to make plans. **T7**

14 Mrs Frisby and the Rats of Nimh
With two thirds of the narrative still to be revealed, new characters are still being introduced, and the plot is gaining mystery and complications. Is this of benefit? **T7**

Investigate connectives, and where they are placed in the sentence ('then'; 'still'; 'suddenly'; 'except that'; 'as if'; 'so'). Identify the range of purposes of connectives. **S4**

Ask the children to make necessary revisions to their plans from Text 13 and to begin their narratives. Allocate time for completion. **T7**

15 When Hitler Stole Pink Rabbit
Can you tell that this is near the end of the book? (Ends tied up; explanations given.) Discuss familiar stories and their endings. Stress the value of clear planning. **T7**

Revise connectives, identifying examples ('afterwards'; 'after all'). Provide examples of connecting phrases, and classify them. Which ones are suitable for which kinds of text? ('Therefore' denotes logic.) Ask the children to find alternatives for supplied connectives, using reading material and a thesaurus. **S4**

16 The Sheep-Pig (2)
Stress the number of simple sentences. Create complex sentences, trying out different connecting devices. Is the meaning still clear? Which link is best? **S5**

This is near the end of the book. Is the ending conventional? (Everything works out well and happily; no problems remain.) How would you have finished it? **T7**

Discuss themes for the children's narratives. Ask them to plan the plot, character and structure; stress the need to think about the ending in advance. **T7**

> **Speaking and listening**
>
> Discuss what the children have learned about narrative planning, using appropriate terminology.
>
> Stress the need for events to be linked.

TERM 2

Poetry

17 Jabberwocky
Read the poem aloud. Share interpretations of nonsense words. Stress that the reader is free to make personal interpretations. **T4**

Analyse mood. Do you all respond in the same way? Experiment in small groups with readings; stress the need to consider pace and intonation. **T5**

Do research on Lewis Carroll and his writing; compare this poem with his others. **T9**

18 The Witches' Chant
Do the children recognise this? (*The Witches* by Roald Dahl.) Consider how to read the poem. Do the words and punctuation indicate growing volume to match the growing threats? Stress the importance of rhythm and sound; evocative use of language; manipulation of words ('grrrowing'; 'frrreaks'). Which words are memorable? **T3**

Ask the children to investigate how Dahl projects humour through this poem. **T4**

19 Fire, Burn; and Cauldron, Bubble
This is the Witches' spell chant in *Macbeth*. Ask the children to study Shakespeare's poetic structure, sound, and use of words. Share findings (rhyming couplets; alliteration; repetition; onomatopoeia). **T3**

Focus on rhythm. How should lines be said? Analyse mood. Is there a growing air of menace and threat? How do you respond? How does the mood compare to Dahl's? **T5**

> **Speaking and listening**
>
> Share group presentations of 'Jabberwocky'. Compare interpretations.
>
> Talk about past poets. Explore and clarify meanings.

Teaching Notes and Ideas

Narrative 1

20 Charlotte Sometimes (1)
How is the passing of time conveyed in the first sentence? ('Next morning…') What else has happened? (Charlotte has gone back in time.) Consider how this theme is handled, identifying details that convey the time movement to the reader (different surroundings; new name). **T1**

Revise complex sentences. Identify examples. Use some as models for the children's own sentences; stress the need for appropriate punctuation. **S3**

21 Charlotte Sometimes (2)
(This carries straight on from the previous text.) Point out that the writer continues to handle the time movement by changing details. Which details are important? (Bell; clothes; suitable names; appropriate language.) **T1**

What does the title tell you? (Charlotte is not always Clare.) Ask the children to carry on writing the story, moving to a later time of the day, when Charlotte returns to the modern age. **T11**

22 The Borrowers
Mrs May's use of the past tense and the word 'nowadays' shows that the character is remembering past events. This is the end of the first chapter. What will probably follow? (The reader is taken through the hole, into the Borrowers' world.) What other books use this device? (In *Carrie's War* the book begins and ends with an adult Carrie; in the rest of the book, she is back in her childhood.) **T1**

Investigate ways in which clauses have been connected in complex sentences. Give practice in identifying main clauses. **S3**

Ask the children to plan a narrative, using a flashback or a story within a story. **T11**

23 Alice Through the Looking Glass
Point out how chapters are linked smoothly (repetition of a verb; continuation of a sentence). What has been happening before this? (Alice has been dreaming.) Why are dreams a useful device? (They allow movement between time periods; add mystery and intrigue; can contain a story within a story.) Do the children like this device? **T1**

Return to the children's narrative plans. Suggest they discuss ideas with a response partner. Allow plenty of time for the final writing. **T11**

24 The Story of Zoe
Is this well-written? Are the children reminded of another story? (Cinderella.) Do the children recognise that it has become silly, a parody of the original version. Why? (Stock characters and plot.) Let the children write parodies of a text. **T13**

Speaking and listening
Focus on the theme of time. Share reading experiences.

Use the texts of *Charlotte Sometimes* for role-play. Let the class return to a former age while a 'Charlotte' character is out of the room. Can the others sustain their parts? What are their new names? How will 'Charlotte' cope when she returns? Use the role-play to stress the need for consistency within a narrative, use of the right verb tense, and the need for the reader to understand.

Teaching Notes and Ideas

Narrative 2

25 What Katy Did (1)

What goes wrong for Katy before reaching school? Analyse how the writer conveys Katy's growing feelings of frustration with each paragraph piling up these feelings ('ran about searching'; 'banging doors'; 'hastily sticking it in'; 'impatient horse'; 'rushed like a whirlwind'; 'very cross mood'). How does the writer want the reader to feel? Is she successful? **T2, T8**

This book was written in the nineteenth century. How is this apparent? (Vocabulary; references; formality.) Can the children find out more about this writer? **T9**

26 Five Children and It

Are the children familiar with this author? (*Classworks Fiction and Poetry Texts Year 4* has extracts from two more of her books.) Ask the children to find out more about Nesbit and when this book was written. **T9**

Discuss responses to this text (interest; excitement; curiosity; suspense). How are these evoked? (Strange happenings; peculiar creatures; odd names; 'impossible' conversations.) Is the writer successful? How do you respond? **T8**

27 Shadow of the Minotaur (1)

This is the end of Chapter 1. Do the children want to read on? This book won the 'Book I couldn't put down' award. Debate characteristics needed for this award: drama; action; compelling characters; tension; suspense. Which characteristics are in this text? Focus on suspense. Analyse how it is built-up: who is he? where is he? will he escape? **T8**

Stress the sequence of sentences and paragraphs following the character's shifting thoughts, as he becomes more afraid. Note the italicised, single line paragraph indicating his thoughts and feeling of desperation. **T2**

28 What Katy Did (2)

Remind the children of the end of Text 25. How did the writer want her reader to feel at that point? (Wondering what would happen during the day; concern for Katy.)

Focus on this new text. Analyse how the writer builds-up suspense, as more incidents occur. Which words reinforce suspense and growing feelings of despair? **T2, T8**

29 Five Children and It (2)

Which genre does the book belong to? (Fantasy.) Which other text in the unit belongs in that category? (*Shadow of the Minotaur*.) What do you expect of such books? This was written in 1902. Are any elements still typical of modern fantasy literature? (Granting of wishes; time travel; unrecognisable creature; appearance changes.) **T7**

Consider how the period is reflected (servants; dress; speech). Analyse the writer's style and use of paragraphs and punctuation. Revise and identify complex sentences. How are clauses connected? Which is the main clause? Model write further examples. **S3**

Brainstorm ideas of what should happen next in this story. Ask the children to write an additional part, retaining the text's language conventions and style. **T12**

30 Shadow of the Minotaur (2)

This continues almost straight on from Text 27. Which old questions posed are now answered? (The character's name.) Which new ones are posed? (How can this be part of a game?) Has the story gained interest? Why? **T8**

TEACHING NOTES AND IDEAS

Why does Phoenix dislike Brownleigh? Investigate where and how the writer reveals the reasons. Point out the strengthening of language. **T2**

Ask the children to plan a piece of extended writing in this genre. Allow ample time for planning, revision and re-drafting. Hold a speaking and listening session during these processes, for children to clarify and organise their thoughts. **T12**

> ## Speaking and listening
> What holds your interest in a book? How can a writer make **you** respond? Use discussion to further children's understanding of authors' techniques.

TERM 3

Reading and writing narrative

31 Moon Cake
This is from the middle of the story. How is the opening paragraph linked to the preceding one? ('The next day…') Investigate the ways other paragraphs are linked (mention of a different character; new thoughts or events; repetition of a word just used; connectives). **T21**

Talk about text annotation. What would you find useful for studying this text? (Descriptive passages; revelations about Tom's personality; focus on one character; simple sentences.) Model annotation of a section. **T7**

Ask the children to continue writing the story; emphasise the importance of sequencing and linking paragraphs. **T21**

32 Dawlish Dobson
Ask the children to make a close reading of the text. Then pose oral questions about content, encouraging the children to now use skimming and scanning to confirm answers quickly and efficiently. **T18**

Revise passive verbs. Identify examples ('be persuaded and cajoled'; 'had been considered'; 'walked'; 'was shattered'). Discuss their effect: a formal, impersonal tone. Compare them with the active verbs used for the characters' speech. **S3**

Ask the children to plan and begin writing a narrative about the first day at a new school. Stress: some use of the passive voice; effective use of paragraphs; appropriate links between paragraphs.

33 The Journey
Focus on writing style. Stress passive verbs and the formal, impersonal tone given. Ask the children to identify examples.

Investigate sentence construction. Ask the children to create complex sentences, by trying different linking devices. **S3**

Give the children time to complete the writing begun with Text 31.

> ## Speaking and listening
> Compare the links chosen for the sentence level work in Text 33. Which connectives work best? What is their impact?
>
> Analyse possible question types, and consider response structures.

Poetry

34 from Annus Mirabilis
Give the children time to read this before discussing it. It is about the Great Fire of London. What is the overall impact? What response are readers left with? Consider how the poet maintains the metaphor of the fire being a devouring monster. Ask the children to trace the development of the theme and the language. **T4**

35 Again
Why is this called 'Again'? (Repeating cycle of seasons.) Investigate how the theme tracks the end of one summer to the return of the next. Compare the 'shrinking' verbs of the first verse to the 'awakening' ones of the second. What is the mood? Is it constant? What is the overall impact? How are you left feeling? **T4**

36 The Road Not Taken
Consider the more complicated rhyme pattern. Does it contribute to mood? What mood is inspired in you? Which words are relevant? **T4**

Analyse meaning. Is a deeper message implied? Suggest that the roads are life decisions: in the future, the poet may regret decisions he has made. **T6**

37 The Donkey
Let the children work in pairs to generate questions to set to the poem and its themes. Do your questions work? What can you discover about the development of this theme? What do you think the overall impact of the poem is? **T4**

> **Speaking and listening**
>
> Share ideas on questions (Text 37). Collaborate on a final list.
>
> Share critical comments on the impact of the language of 'The Donkey'.

Robert Louis Stevenson

38 Escape at Bedtime
Give the children time to read this to one another. What is the main subject? (Stars.) What is the structure? (Alternating rhyme pattern.)

Use the term 'personification'. Point out the integration of people and stars. Which verbs do you expect to be applied to stars? ('glittered'; 'shone'.) Which words apply normally to people? ('winked'; 'saw'; 'chased'.)

Revise the distinction between a simile and a metaphor. Point out the word 'as' ('As the crowds…') introducing a simile. **T4**

39 The Moon
Put the children into small groups to analyse content, style and structure. Ask them to make notes, in preparation for a class discussion.

Mention rhyming couplets; simile; rhythm. Is there a link with the previous poem? (Focus on the night sky; regularity in rhythm and rhyme; simile.) **T2**

Can the children comment on Stevenson's style? How do they evaluate it? Provide an opportunity for research on this poet and his work. **T3**

Teaching Notes and Ideas

Emily Dickinson

40 The Moon
Compare this with Text 39. Which poem do you prefer? Ask the children to describe Dickinson's style, rhyme pattern, use of simile, metaphor and personification. How do you respond to the poem? **T2, T3**

Ask the children to begin a cycle of poems about the evening sky. Discuss forms. **T13**

41 Evening
Point out the importance of imagery, as remnants of the day are tidied up into a night sky. Which words support this image? Compare this with the previous text. How would you describe Dickinson's style? **T3**

> **Speaking and listening**
>
> Discuss key elements in the styles of these poets. Are they similar or different? Which poem(s) do you prefer? Why? Point out the relevance of personal response.
>
> Encourage children to share other poems on this theme.

Authors and texts

42 Black Beauty
Ask the children to investigate sentence construction and punctuation preferences. Does the style suit the story? Does the style have strengths and weaknesses? **T1**

Sewell draws attention to the use and treatment of horses. What are her views? Do her views strengthen or weaken her writing? Ask the children to write a summary of the points she draws attention to. **T9**

43 Why the Whales Came (2)
Analyse the different attitudes shown to the whales. Is an animal being used to reflect opposing human attitudes and superstitions? Ask for a written summary of the points Morpurgo makes. Ask the children to identify complex sentences. Experiment with the manipulation of clauses. What difference is made to the text? **S4**

Michael Morpurgo would be an interesting writer to use for a deeper study of style. Texts 5 and 47 are further examples of his work. **T1**

44 The Mouse and his Child
What are the children's responses to this text? How does the style compare with Text 42? (This text has very detailed descriptions; more sophisticated language; both writers favour the use of semicolons.) Which do you prefer? Why? **T6, T12**

Model a layout, first asking the children to record their responses to this text in their reading journals, in preparation for a future discussion. Focus on the importance of writing style suiting subject matter as well as audience. **T8**

45 Magnus Powermouse
Focus on Madeleine's language. Why is it difficult to understand? (Local dialect.) Which words or grammatical constructions are not standard English? How would they be expressed by Marcus Aurelius? Discuss dialect words common to your region. Are many in popular use? Research among older relatives, or interviews conducted in a small community, could produce an interesting collection. **S2**

Compare this with the style of writing in King-Smith's other books (Texts 6 and 16). **T5**

46 The Amazing Maurice and his Educated Rodents

How are animals viewed? (Seriously? Sympathetically? As equals? As superior?) How do you respond? Evaluate the likely appeal of the text; ask the children to prepare for discussion by recording responses in reading journals. **T1, T8**

Analyse writing style. Stress the clear depiction of Maurice's character, allowing the reader to share the cat's thoughts. Investigate sentence constructions and punctuation. Manipulate clauses, perhaps creating a complex sentence from a number of simpler sentences. Compare the result with Pratchett's style. Is the effect different? Does a staccato style suit Maurice's personality? **S4**

Write a summary of the incidents that made him realise he was amazing. **T9**

> ### Speaking and listening
> Hold a discussion on Text 44, based on observations in reading journals.
> What have the children found out about Michael Morpurgo's work?

Extended narrative

47 The War of Jenkins' Ear
Discuss what is happening. Who is probably the main character? (Jenkins – because of the book's title.) Ask the children to read the blurb on the back cover of their present reading books. What could you say about this book? **T10**

48 Harry Potter and the Order of the Phoenix
How is this text linked to the previous extract? (School story.) Discuss differences: plentiful supply of delicious food; unusual names and references; noise and cheerfulness. Do you know the story? Discuss Rowling's previous books. Ask the children to write back cover blurb for one of them. **T10**

Provide access to some book reviews. Point out that reviewers give insight into books, without revealing too much. Ask the children to consider books they have read this year, perhaps focusing on books in your classroom collection. Put the children in pairs to collaborate on writing short reviews for next year's class. **T11**

49 Changing Places
Stress the focus on Emma. Ask the children to list what they learn about her in this extract. Investigate how past and future problems are hinted at. How is the story likely to proceed? Ask the children to write a brief synopsis of the text. **T10**

50 Goodnight Mr Tom
When do you think this is set? (Second World War.) Are there any clues? (Evacuees.) Does Willie enjoy school?

Discuss the enduring popularity of school stories, and ask the children to begin initial plans for their own extended narratives on this theme. Allow time for oral work, in which the children can test their ideas on a response partner. **T14**

> ### Speaking and listening
> Discuss one of this year's class novels. Collaborate on writing a review.
> Listen to reviews written after Text 48.
>
> Prepare reviews of books the children want to recommend to a younger class.
> Visit the class so that the children can make oral presentations.